#12343523

P9-CDE-714

HERMES BOOKS

John Herington, General Editor

AESCHYLUS

JOHN HERINGTON

YALE UNIVERSITY PRESS
NEW HAVEN AND LONDON

Designed by Sally Harris
and set in Palatino type by
Brevis Press, Bethany, Connecticut.
Printed in the United States of America by
Vail-Ballou Press, Binghamton, New York.

Library of Congress Cataloging-in-Publication Data

Herington, C. J.
  Aeschylus.

  (Hermes books)
  Bibliography: p.
  Includes index.
  I. Aeschylus—Criticism and interpretation. I. Title.
PA3829.H45   1986   882'.01   85–14590
ISBN 0–300–03562–4 (alk. paper)

The paper in this book meets the guidelines for
permanence and durability of the Committee on
Production Guidelines for Book Longevity
of the Council on Library Resources.

10   9   8   7   6   5   4   3   2   1

CONTENTS

FOREWORD

"It would be a pity," said nietzsche, "if the classics should speak to us less clearly because a million words stood in the way." His forebodings seem now to have been realized. A glance at the increasing girth of successive volumes of the standard journal of classical bibliography, *L'Année Philologique*, since World War II is enough to demonstrate the proliferation of writing on the subject in our time. Unfortunately, the vast majority of the studies listed will prove on inspection to be largely concerned with points of detail and composed by and for academic specialists in the field. Few are addressed to the literate but nonspecialist adult or to that equally important person, the intelligent but uninstructed beginning student; and of those few, very few indeed are the work of scholars of the first rank, equipped for their task not merely with raw classical erudition but also with style, taste, and literary judgment.

It is a strange situation. On one side stand the classical masters of Greece and Rome, those models of concision, elegance, and understanding of the human condition, who composed least of all for narrow technologists, most of all for the Common Reader (and, indeed, the Common Hearer). On the other side stands a sort of industrial complex, processing those masters into an annually growing output of technical articles and monographs. What is lacking, it seems, in our society as well as in our scholarship, is the kind of book that was supplied for earlier generations by such men as Richard Jebb and Gilbert Murray in the intervals of their more technical researches—the kind of book that directed the general reader not to the pyramid of secondary literature piled over the burial places of the classical writers but to the living faces of the writers themselves, as perceived by a scholar-humanist with a deep knowledge of, and love for, his subject. Not only for the sake of the potential student of classics, but also for the sake of the humanities as a whole, within and outside academe, it seems that this gap in classical studies ought to be filled. The Hermes series is a modest attempt to fill it.

We have sought men and women possessed of a rather rare combination of qualities: a love for literature in other languages, extending into modern times; a vision that extends beyond academe to contemporary life itself; and above all an ability to express themselves in clear, lively, and graceful English, without polysyllabic language or parochial jargon. For the aim of the series requires that they should communicate to nonspecialist readers, authoritatively and vividly, their personal sense of why a given classical author's writings have excited people for centuries and why they can continue to do so. Some are classical scholars by profession, some are not; each has lived long with the classics, and especially with the author about whom he or she writes in this series.

The first, middle, and last goal of the Hermes series is to guide the general reader to a dialogue with the classical masters rather than to acquaint him or her with the present state of scholarly research. Thus our volumes contain few or no footnotes; even within the texts, references to secondary literature are kept to a minimum. At the end of each volume, however, is a short bibliography that includes recommended English translations, and selected literary criticism, as well as historical and (when appropriate) biographical studies.

In these ways we hope to let the classics speak again, with a minimum of modern verbiage (as Nietzsche wished), to the widest possible audience of interested people.

All the translations from Aeschylus' plays and fragments that will be found in this book are my own. I have translated into prose where close exposition of Aeschylus' literal sense seemed desirable, into verse (and somewhat more freely) where I felt that the uppermost need was to convey, however inadequately, the feel of the poetry.

John Herington

PROLOGUE

City and Earth and shining Water,
And Gods of highest heaven,
And Gods deep-honored under ground
Who hold the tombs,
And Zeus, third, Savior!

Joining the reader in an approach to the mysterious
territory of Aeschylus, I open with words chanted by one of
his choruses as it moves into the theater (*Suppliants* 23–26).
The chorus-members, too, have newly landed in a strange
country. Their greeting to it, so unlike any greeting that might
be expected of a modern traveler, seems to gather up into one
sentence the Aeschylean vision of our world. They invoke the
entire environment—human, divine, and (as we, but not the
early Greeks, would put it) inanimate. Ranked side by side,
with impartial reverence, are the political community, the natural elements, the powers of the bright sky, the powers of the
dark earth who hold the dead in their keeping, and finally
the god whom Aeschylus most often names, Zeus.

To enter imaginatively into that word-vision seems a necessary preliminary to understanding, and delighting in, the
plays of Aeschylus. Until two or three decades ago this was
not easy for Westerners. *Analysis*, the dissolution of the observed world and of life itself into separately intelligible units,
has been our great achievement. The early Greek sense of

1

wholeness, of a world whose parts, spiritual and material, were interdependent and possessed equal power for good or ill, had long been lost. Only slowly and painfully are we beginning to relearn, from the ecologists, how the survival of all life depends on an uncertain balance of forces natural and moral, among them human greed. Once more our physicians, like their ancient Greek predecessors, are considering the need to treat the patient as a physiological and psychological unity, the condition of which partly depends on its environment. And most people probably understand by now that the ultimate catastrophe of nuclear war will, if it happens, result simultaneously from the unseen depths of matter and from the unseen depths of human passion. We may therefore be in a better position now than people have been in for many centuries to grasp the Aeschylean universe.

That will be our first consideration in this book. The second will be the playwright himself and the times through which he lived. At that point in the enquiry, we may begin to understand why he represented our universe in the way he did, and why no Greek poet or prose writer after him was ever able to reproduce a similar vision. An account of his unique medium, the Athenian theater, will follow; finally, in Part 2, we shall arrive at the reason for this book's existence: the poetic dramas of Aeschylus.

PART I

BACKGROUND TO AESCHYLUS' WORK

I THE WORLD-VISION

IT SHOULD BE UNDERSTOOD THAT "AESCHYLUS' WORLD-VISION," here and throughout the book, is simply a short way of saying "the world-vision deducible from Aeschylus' plays." As will be seen in chapter 2, the evidence for the career and personal opinions of Aeschylus the man is even scantier than the evidence for those of Shakespeare the man. We are hardly in any position to affirm what Aeschylus himself believed. At most, we may guess that a vision presented so consistently and expounded with such passion over so long a time is unlikely to have been a vision from which he felt utterly distanced in his non-working hours. But whether or nor that is so, here are the most prominent features of the world that emerges from the plays.

Olympians

To the reader, now poised on the perimeter of the Aeschylean universe and surveying the scene within, one shining group of figures may not seem too unfamiliar, at least on a distant view: the family of the Olympian gods. They have been with our civilization at least since Homer composed his *Iliad* and *Odyssey* in the eighth century B.C., and probably—if we rightly reconstruct the ancient preliterate tradition in which Homer must have been bred—since long before then. In a sense the Olympians are not dead even at this hour.

Although they were never very well adapted to respond to the deepest religious needs of humanity, they have always responded superbly—long after their temples have collapsed in ruins—to its imaginative and artistic needs. For they are essentially vast shadows of ourselves. Despite their power and immortality, they have enough humanity in them to serve as brilliant patterns for most human characters and relationships. If the Greek artist, or the Italian Renaissance artist, would show our nature writ large in either its better aspects or its worse, the Olympian family was always there at his disposal.

All the members of this family are present and potent in the universe created by Aeschylus' plays: most notably the Father, Zeus, his wife, Hera, and his children Apollo, Artemis, and Athena. On the whole they have the attributes, functions, and personal histories that are familiar to us from Homer (and Ovid, and Rubens; one could extend the list, of course, well into the nineteenth century); but there are two important differences in Aeschylus' perception of them. First, he is far more conscious than Homer is of their respective links with specific Greek sanctuaries and cults, such as Hera's at Argos, Apollo's at Delphi, and Athena's on the Athenian Acropolis; in this aspect of presiding deity of a great shrine an Olympian takes on another dimension, becoming a more solemn, more truly religious figure than he or she can normally be in an epic poem. Second, especially in Aeschylus' later plays, Zeus acquires attributes that are unlike, and even inconsistent with, the attributes of Homer's Olympian gods. Aeschylus reproduces many of the ancient myths which show Zeus in his all too human or even his bestial aspects—his rape, in bull form, of the virgin Io, for instance—and yet he is equally capable of perceiving the god as he does in the following couplet, preserved from his lost play *Heliades* ("The Daughters of the Sun"; fragment S 34*):

> Zeus is air, and Zeus is earth, and Zeus is sky—
> Zeus is all things, and all beyond the all!

There is an extraordinary tension here between the ancient and what would appear to be, for Aeschylus' time, the very new. It will be explored further in the final chapter.

Elemental Powers

In Aeschylus' universe the gods who hold Olympus are by no means the only powers that we transient mortals have to respect and contend with. Divinity also reigns around us and below us—divinity equally potent, and often all the more formidable because it does not usually manifest itself in the clear-cut, accessible human forms of the Olympians. Earth, Sky, Ocean, and Sun are all mighty gods in this universe. To slight them may attract a terrible vengeance, as the invaders of Greece discovered in Aeschylus' *Persians*—and as the industrialized nations are painfully rediscovering in the twentieth century. Even lesser natural objects in Aeschylus seem to possess, if not exactly divinity, at least a rich life of their own. For example, here is the Persian Queen's description of the offerings she makes at her husband's tomb (*Persians* 611–18):

> The sweet white milk of an unblemished cow;
> And honey-drops, gift of the Flower-Reaper,
> Light-drenched; and water from a maiden spring;

---

*For the system of reference to the fragments of Aeschylus' lost plays, see the Bibliographical Epilogue.

And here, pure drink from a mother in the wilds—
The liquid glory of an ancient vine;
And here, the scented fruit of an olive-tree
Golden, exulting in her undying leaves;
And here are woven flowers,
Children of Earth, who nurtures all that is.

Earth-Powers

In Aeschylus' world, just as in ours, Earth "brings all
things to birth, and nurtures them, and in turn takes back to
herself what she has grown" (*Libation-Bearers* 127–28); she fos-
ters the living, and she is keeper of the dead. But it is doubtful
whether the modern urban imagination is more than fitfully
conscious even of that basic and inexorable fact. To the early
Greeks, however, and especially to the speakers in Aeschylus'
plays, Earth is ever present as a powerful divinity; and, with
her, not only the plants and animals which rise from her surface but also the teeming occupants of her depths. She herself, in most early Greek poetry, *knows* and *is* rather than *does*.
She is simply there, a feminine principle older than the patriarchal Olympians and on some issues far wiser than they.
Associated with her are many other feminine powers: Night,
Moira or the *Moirai* ("Fate" or "Fates"), and the *Erinyes* (meaning, apparently, something like "Ragers" but usually translated as "Furies"; sometimes we find them referred to in the
singular, *Erinys*). Of these, the Erinyes tend to intervene most
directly in human affairs; for their business is to enforce the
ancient and unchanging prerogatives of the Earth-Powers
generally, and in particular of the dead.

With the dead, and above all with the dead ancestors of
any given individual, we arrive at one of the most powerful
influences in the Aeschylean universe. To assimilate this con-

cept, again, most modern city-dwellers will have to readjust their imaginations considerably, although there may be exceptions among the geneticists. Not through scientific observation, of course, but through the practical experience of a social organization that had centered for untold generations on the *clan*, the early Greeks possessed a most acute sense of the extent to which a human being may be programmed for good or ill by his heredity—how the characteristics of the long dead may still haunt him and his behavior. The idea of the family curse, so notorious an element in many of the most famous Greek legends, seems to be but one expression of this sense. Where the early Greeks part company from most modern secular feeling (Christianity, especially Catholic Christianity, is another matter) is in their belief that we can make contact with the dead members of our families and influence them. One cannot, that I know of, placate the Double Helix. In Aeschylus, however, a dead father may be as powerful a presence as a live one, or more so. As Orestes stands at the tomb of the murdered Agamemnon, the Chorus warns him (*Libation-Bearers* 324–26):

> My child, the dead man's will
> Cannot be tamed in the ravening maw of fire
> But in a later day reveals its rage.

Where or in what guise the dead exist it would be hard to say, in Aeschylus' time as in ours. Early Greek tomb-rituals, not only in drama but also in actual practice, implied that somehow the spirit still lingered in the tomb. The family would place offerings and eat meals there, and they might even pour libations through a hole that led to the corpse itself. Yet at the same time both popular and poetic belief also acknowledged the existence of a realm beneath Earth's surface where all "the famous nations of the dead" (in Homer's

phrase) were gathered together. This realm is in some ways
a sinister mirror-image of the realm of light. It too is ruled by
a divine wedded couple. As Olympian Zeus and Hera reign
in the sky, so under Earth reign Hades—whom Aeschylus
calls "earth-Zeus, . . . Zeus of the dead" in *The Suppliants*
156–58—and sad Persephone.

Living Humanity

What is the status of a mere human being who walks the
world that we have described so far? At first sight it might
seem that he or she is destined to be a mere victim: the inert
solution to a monstrously complicated equation of those vast
and varied divine forces, supernal and infernal. But here we
return to an aspect of Aeschylus' universe that seems to be
of central importance. *This is a universe in which everything
matters and everything interacts.* And "everything" includes, as
it must, living men and women.

At dead center of the *Oresteia,* Aeschylus has his chorus
pause from the action and reflect. The details of the Greek
text are uncertain, especially toward the end of the first of the
two stanzas that I shall quote, but the general drift is clear:
the singers are matching the powers of what moderns would
call the physical universe against the powers hidden within
the human soul (*Libation-Bearers* 585–601):

> Our Earth is mother
> Of many a cruel horror.
> Teeming in the ocean's arms
> Swim monsters enemies to man.
> Lightning blossoms, hanging
> In the no-man's-land of sky.
> Bird and beast alike could tell
> of the hurricane's stormy spite.

But *who* could tell
Of Man's over-daring will?
And the bold loves in Woman's heart,
All-daring loves, cohabiting
With human doom?
For female love unloving
Would conquer all, subverting
Shared dens of monsters and of men.

Humanity also is a great power in Aeschylus' universe, too often, indeed (but not always), for evil. In the later of his surviving plays, and above all in the *Oresteia*, mere human actions and passions may be seen as ultimately shaking the entire fabric of that universe, as dividing the ultimate powers of Earth and Sky themselves.

Reflections on the Dramatization of the Universe

This short tour through the universe envisaged in Aeschylus' plays is designed only for preliminary orientation; many more details, as well as some qualifications, are reserved for Part 2. Here, however, it may be worth pausing to review certain consequences of what we have seen. It has already been suggested that some aspects, at least, of that universe are not so remote from our contemporary experience of reality as they might seem to be at first sight. Underlying the ancient metaphorical, mythical, and religious language in which Aeschylus necessarily expressed himself appear to be insights into our world that might still make good sense to a contemporary geneticist, environmentalist, or, indeed, psychologist. Furthermore, that language seems capable of relating all the phenomena of life. Any human being's existence, at any date, is conditioned and limited externally by the family, the society, the landscape, and the climate in which he lives; internally, by his heredity and by the constant tension between the clear, bright images created in his conscious mind and the dark, unanalyzable forces that well up from the unconscious. The majestic totality of those factors in human behavior may perhaps be more easily and effectively represented to the mind in the ancient mythical language—once its grammar and syntax have been relearned—than it actually is through the discrete languages and sublanguages that have been generated by the various modern sciences.

Granted, in any case, that the world-vision of Aeschylus and the language available to him in which to represent it were such as have been described, we may address the final question to be considered in this chapter: under such conditions, *what kind of a drama can one compose?* By the standards to which the Western theater became accustomed from the time of Aeschylus' great successor in the tragic art, Sophocles, until the end of the nineteenth century, the answer to that question would seem to be *no drama at all.* Sophocles and the majority of the dramatists who followed him for many centuries tended to focus their plays on clearly outlined and defined individuals, visible onstage. In the growing revelation of those individuals' characters through speech and action, in the interplay of their wills and passions, in the mounting suspense as to the outcome, in the dénouement that finally determined their natures and their fates, lay—and lies—the fascination of that dramatic mode. Yet in the Aeschylean world-vision it is just not possible to isolate a human being in such a way, to disentangle him or her artificially from the seamless web of the material and spiritual universe. It is equally impossible to envisage a given sequence of events as due solely to the interaction of a handful of human, or even divine, individuals. Aeschylean drama, on the contrary, is

occupied with the interaction of all the forces that make up
our world, all between the dome of heaven and the recesses
of hell. Humanity is but one of those forces; of the non-hu-
man, some are introduced into the plot by the sheer force of
verbal poetry; others actually materialize, masked and costumed, in the theater.

This is a dramatic mode that for ages after Aeschylus'
death became wholly or partially unintelligible to the literate
public, as Western civilization developed along the lines it
did. His poetry never ceased to be marveled at; but his plays
never seem to have been restaged by the Greeks or Romans
after about 400 B.C. and were scarcely ever treated seriously,
as *plays*, by the later classical critics. Here and there, indeed,
as one looks down the entire span of twenty-four centuries
that separates us from Aeschylus, one may make out a temporary recurrence of this mode in some form or another: in
the tragedies of the Roman Seneca in the first century A.D.;
in some of the mediaeval miracle-plays; perhaps in one or two
Jacobean tragedies. Yet the most spectacular recurrence of all
seems to be discernible in our own century. The Theater of
the Absurd, for instance, has somewhat similarly opened up
the focus of drama to scan not merely the human individual
but also the complex of mysterious phenomena that surround
and interact with him. Antonin Artaud, indeed, devised an
influential program for a twentieth-century drama (he called
it the Theater of the Cruel) which in some ways comes quite
close to the Aeschylean mode. A few extracts from his *The
Theater and Its Double* (see the Epilogue for the bibliographical
details) may in fact serve very well to put a spectator in the
right frame of mind before taking his seat in the theater of
Aeschylus:

> Everyday loves, personal ambition, struggles for status,
> all have value only in proportion to their relation to the

terrible lyricism of the Myths to which the great mass of men have assented. [p. 85]

Manikins, enormous masks, objects of strange proportions, will appear with the same sanction as verbal images. [p. 97]

The Theater of Cruelty will choose subjects and themes corresponding to the agitation and unrest characteristic of our epoch. . . . These themes will be cosmic, universal, and interpreted according to the most ancient texts drawn from old Mexican, Hindu, Judaic, and Iranian cosmogonies. Renouncing psychological man, with his well-directed character and feelings, submissive to laws and misshapen by religions and precepts, the Theater of Cruelty will address itself only to total man. And it will cause not only the recto but the verso of the mind to play its part; the reality of imagination and dreams will appear there on equal footing with life. [pp. 122–23]

It will stage events, not men. Men will come in their turn with their psychology and their passions, but they will be taken as the emanation of certain forces and understood in the light of the events and historical fatality in which they have played their role. [p. 126]

II THE POET
IN HIS TIME

The Great Transition

TO THE ATHENIAN SOCIETY INTO WHICH AESCHYLUS WAS
born, about 525 B.C., the ancient mythic vision outlined in
chapter 1 must have been completely familiar. For untold centuries, not only they and their fellow Greeks but also the
peoples of the Near East and of India had perceived and accounted for the world in some such terms, however much the
details might have varied from place to place. The myths offered the only available language in which ideas about human
life above the level of day-to-day business could be expressed,
whether in verse, in painting, or in sculpture. But during the
last decades of Aeschylus' life that society, and with it that
language, were being transformed with an abruptness absolutely unparalleled in the ancient world, whether Greek or
Eastern. In some important respects, our own civilization was
emerging, and the ancient world-vision was beginning to disintegrate under its impact. It is hard to measure the world-
historical significance of that collapse. Geological analogies
might be found in those natural catastrophes that seem to
occur every so many million years, obliterating entire life-
systems. On the far smaller scale of human history, some
analogies might be found in the European Renaissance; yet
even more might be found in our own era. We do not know
from year to year what the age of mass civilization and high

15

technology may bring: whether a richer earth and a richer humanity, or no earth and no humanity at all. And whatever the change awaiting us, will our values or even our gods survive it? Different as our present transition obviously is in many details from that experienced by Aeschylus' Athens, its basic psychological effects seem quite similar. Today we share that uncertainty, that sense of dread, that occasional brilliant flare of hope for a coming world.

The uniqueness of Aeschylean drama seems to reside in this: it is expressed almost entirely in the immemorially old mythic-poetic idiom in which Aeschylus—and, no doubt, the great majority of his audiences—had been raised; and yet it is heavily (in the latest plays one might even say *desperately*) engaged with the Athenian transition to a new world, a world that in many senses is still ours.

Aeschylus in a Changing Athens

Because the art of biography was not yet known in Aeschylus' lifetime, or indeed for several lifetimes after, no reliable record survives of his inner life, and little of his external career. The most solid evidence for the latter is derived from the official Athenian records of the annual dramatic performances; extracts from those records, preserved by later Greek scholars, show that Aeschylus first produced a drama in ca. 498 B.C. and was still active in the Athenian theater as late as 458. During that long period he composed well over eighty dramas. (The exact total is uncertain, but eighty-nine is the likeliest figure on the evidence we have.) Of these, only seven have survived complete out of the general destruction of classical literature that accompanied the collapse of the Roman Empire.

In this chapter I shall bring together what little else is

recorded (with varying degrees of certainty) about the poet and his career; and concurrently I shall sketch the momentous changes that were taking place in the city of Athens during Aeschylus' long life. (For a summary, see the Table of Dates at the end of the book.)

The family into which he was born in about 525 B.C. was an ancient and aristocratic one, settled in the town of Eleusis, some fourteen miles northwest of the city of Athens. It may be a significant biographical fact in itself that the chief glory of Eleusis was its sanctuary of the Great Goddesses, Demeter and her daughter Persephone (whom we have already encountered as Queen of Hades). There, from time immemorial, were celebrated the famous Eleusinian Mysteries, with their annual promise of new life for vegetation and for humanity. The living presence of the Earth-Powers could probably be felt more vividly there than on any other Greek site. Otherwise our only material relating to the first three decades of Aeschylus' life are the record of his first dramatic production in ca. 498 B.C. and a legend, which runs as follows: "Aeschylus used to say that once, when he was a teenager, he was guarding the grapes in the countryside and fell asleep. Dionysus appeared standing over him and told him to compose tragedy. When daylight came, since he wanted to obey the god, he tried it, and found it easy from that moment on."

This story, beautiful as it is, is all too probably a much later invention; it is recorded only in an author who wrote six centuries after Aeschylus (Pausanias, *Description of Greece*, 1.21.2), and it bears a suspicious resemblance to a large group of fictions about various great authors by which the postclassical Greeks sought to account for that still mysterious phenomenon, the inspiration of an artist. Yet it is likely enough on grounds of common experience that Aeschylus' interest in the art that was to obsess him for a lifetime should have awakened when he was a teenager. And in any event the year 510 B.C., to which the story approximately points, may be selected as a convenient benchmark for a survey of the Athens in which Aeschylus was growing up.

That year saw the abrupt end of a political regime which had lasted in the city, on and off, for exactly fifty years: the rule (*tyranny* was the term used by contemporaries, but without necessarily the hateful sense the word later acquired) of Pisistratus and his sons. During that half-century the political development of Athens had practically stood still; but the vast and restless energies of the Athenians had been applied to commerce, industry, and the arts, with wonderful effect. Before 560 Athens had been only one among many considerable independent Greek cities that extended over a great arc of the Old World, from Marseilles in the west to the coastline of the Black Sea in the east. By 510 it was on the verge of becoming one of the two most influential Greek communities, the other being the great military power, Sparta. Athenian trade now reached across the entire Greek-occupied area, and beyond. The physical appearance of the city itself, especially the Acropolis, had been transformed. The Pisistratid era had been the first great age of Attic temple-building and large-scale sculpture. On the Acropolis the fifteen-year-old Aeschylus would have walked among two majestic temples of the city-goddess, Athena, and at least half a dozen smaller shrines, all of them built within the last two generations. The roofs were tiled in brilliantly colored terracotta. From the pediments magnificent, and in many cases unearthly, forms carved in stone and painted in many colors looked down: Olympian gods battling Earth's children, the Giants; animal powers in the shapes of outsize lions and bulls, in all their terror; and monsters half human, half snake or fish, perhaps embodying the forces of Earth and Sea. Around the temples stood or sat a great silent population of votive statues in bronze or painted marble. It included monsters, animals, noble horseback riders, and those smiling statues of *korai*—young women—which to this day leave the strongest impression on the visitor to the Acropolis Museum. They are extraordinary—as Aeschylus' poetry was later to be—for their combination of exquisitely crafted surface detail with a stunning sense of life.

The regime of the tyrants had similarly fostered the arts of poetry and music in Athens, partly by establishing contests in them at great religious festivals and partly by inviting famous poet-musicians from all over the Greek world to the city. By 510 B.C. Athens was fast becoming one of the leading centers of Greek poetry and song, just as it was achieving supremacy in the visual arts. The youthful Aeschylus, before the regime fell, could have heard performances there by the great choral lyric poets Simonides and Lasus, and by the equally great solo lyricist Anacreon. Almost certainly he would have attended the poetic and musical contests that were held at Athena's greatest festival, the Panathenaea: contests in the recitation of Homer's *Iliad* and *Odyssey,* in the singing of poetry to the lyre, and in unaccompanied lyre and woodwind music. And one wonders if any force could have kept him away from the Great Dionysia Festival, with its annual contests in a recently developed art form called *tragoidia,* which combined into one overwhelming performance both the poetic and the visual genius of Athens. It was the art of all arts, embracing choral and solo song, lyre and woodwind music, recited poetry, and costume and mask. These tragic contests at the Great Dionysia had been founded as lately as ca. 534 B.C., during the reign of Pisistratus and no doubt with his encouragement or even on his instructions. Of all the achievements of Pisistratus and his dynasty this was to prove the most enduring. Almost all the others proved transient:

his political system, his family of princes, and even the magnificent monuments of his Acropolis were to be swept out of sight within relatively few years. The Dionysiac festival and its effects are with us still.

Thus, the Athens in which Aeschylus spent his childhood and early adolescence represented archaic Greek civilization at its acme. All around him the ancient religious and mythical way of thinking was finding its richest expression, in poetry and visual art alike. In 510 B.C., however, began a series of events, primarily political, which were first to shake and finally to disintegrate that brilliant cultural fabric. In that year the ruling tyrant, Hippias, son of Pisistratus, was expelled from Athens with the rest of his clan. "And Athens, great as she had been before, then, on being rid of her tyrant, became even greater"; such are the words of the earliest Greek historian, Herodotus (5.66.1). Those impetuous Athenian energies were now released in all directions: externally, in wars with several other Greek cities; internally, at first in violent political factions, and then in an unprecedented political experiment, the constitution introduced by the statesman Cleisthenes in about 507 B.C. For our purposes we need not go into the details of that intricate political mechanism (the interested reader may find many of them in accounts by Herodotus, 5.66–69, and in Aristotle, *Constitution of Athens*, 21), but its implications were and are momentous. Earlier statesmen in Athens and elsewhere in Greece had tinkered with this or that feature of the traditional political structures, inherited from time immemorial. Cleisthenes, on the other hand, in effect coolly dismantled the entire fabric and assembled a new one, partly from the old components and partly from components of his own devising. Latent in this achievement was a philosophical and religious, as well as a political, revolution: if man's intellect could thus restructure his social environment at will, what could it *not* restructure in the long run? Even the immediate and obvious political effect, however, seems to mark an epoch in the history of Western civilization. All citizens of Athens were now to be equal before the law, and all were empowered to participate, at least in some degree, in the government of the community. The term used by some Greek writers of this system is *demokratia*. It was not yet a complete democracy in the later Greek sense, still less in the modern one; but both derive from this beginning.

In the years just after 500 B.C., about the time when Aeschylus was producing his earliest plays at the Dionysiac festival, began another chain of events that were to have an incalculable effect on the history of Athens and the life of Aeschylus: the wars between the Greeks and the Persian Empire. Already for about half a century the far-off Persians had expanding beyond their ancient borders, which were roughly those occupied today by their descendants, the Iranians. The ancient kingdoms of the Near East had collapsed one by one before their armies, until by the beginning of the fifth century the Persian King of Kings ruled from the banks of the Indus in the east to Egypt and the Cyrenaica in the southwest, and to Thrace in the northwest. The consolidation of that entire area under a single power was of world-historical importance; its impact is still to be felt in the Bible, for instance, as well as in the writers of Greece and Rome. In their long defiance of that seemingly invincible force, the Greeks, and above all the Athenians, reached maturity and made their entrance onto the world stage.

The main struggle lasted over a period of just twenty years. It began in 499 B.C. with a revolt of the Greek cities along the west coast of Asia Minor that were already tributaries of the Persian Empire. The Persians crushed this rebellion within five years, but not before the ever-venturesome Athenians, joining with the city of Eretria in Euboea, had intervened with a fleet sent to help the rebels. On the surface, at least, it was in revenge for that intervention that in 490 the Persians launched their first expedition against the Greek homeland. A Persian fleet landed first at Eretria and destroyed it. Then it stood on to a harbor called Marathon, on the northeast coast of the Athenian territory. Disembarking there, the Persian troops were charged and routed by the heavily armed Athenian infantry. One of the few fairly certain facts of Aeschylus' personal life is that he fought in the battle-line at that victory. With him there was his brother Cynegei-rus, who was killed in the subsequent rush to seize the Persian ships at the beachhead (Herodotus 6.114).

From then on, Athens and all Greece seemed to lie under sentence of death. The Persian king, Darius, enraged by the defeat at Marathon, began preparations for a massive invasion of Greece by land and sea. Those preparations were set back by his death in 486 B.C. and by the political problems that ensued, but by the spring of 480 his son and successor, Xerxes, set out at the head of the great expedition. In Athens, during the ten-year interval between invasions, the most significant historical event was the construction of a large fleet. All we know of Aeschylus during the same period is that he was back at work in the theater, for the record shows that in 484 he won for the first time in his career the coveted first prize in the dramatic competitions.

The great Persian invasion of 480–479 will be further discussed in chapter 6, in connection with *The Persians*. Here it is enough to recall that in each summer of those two years the Persian host occupied and ravaged the city of Athens. When the defeated Persians finally turned tail and straggled homeward in the fall of 479, the Athenians returned to a chaos of fire-scarred ruins. Physically, the splendors of archaic Athens, the Athens of Aeschylus' youth, were no more. (The reason that we can still reconstruct the general appearance of the Pisistratid Acropolis is that fragments of the temples and sculptures thrown down by the Persians were used as landfill for Pericles' great building program in the years after 450. After that they were not to see the sunlight again until the late nineteenth century, when they were disinterred by the Greek archaeologists.) From that point of view the archaic slate had been wiped clean. And in fact a new Athens was to emerge, not merely physically speaking but also politically and intellectually, during the twenty-three years that Aeschylus had still to live after the final defeat of the Persian invasion. The great transition is manifested directly to the eye in the Athenian sculptures and vase-paintings of the postinvasion years: the style evolves swiftly from the archaic to what art historians call the classic—an artistic language without parallel in earlier periods, whether in Greece or in the Near East, and the precedent for much of European art hereafter. The artist now concentrates on the human form in its dynamic aspect, in its capacity for movement and the expression of moral and intellectual character through movement; correspondingly, he turns away from the animals and monsters that had been such a striking element in the population of the Pisistratid Acropolis (and of the archaic world-vision generally).

For other facets of the great postwar transition we have to turn from the visible monuments to written documents for the most part, but the message of these is equally clear in its own way. A rapid political and economic change took place in Athens—first externally, then internally. Immediately after the defeat of Xerxes, the Athenians used their new fleet to master the shores and islands of the entire Aegean sea. Their mastery at first took the form of a defensive naval league; but by the time of Aeschylus' death it was beginning to resemble a tribute-paying empire; and Athens, the focal point of all this wealth and power, was becoming something that the European mainland had never yet seen, a great urbanized metropolis. Within the last seven years of Aeschylus' life, largely (it seems) in response to the changed economic and social conditions of an imperial Athens, came a massive constitutional change—so massive, and accompanied by such violent factional strife, that it may almost deserve the name of revolution. Under the leadership of a radical group which included the young Pericles, the system inherited from Cleisthenes was restructured in such a way that it now became a full democracy in the Greek sense. From then on, in theory at least, the city, its magistracies, its law courts, and its destiny were under the control of the vast majority of the citizens, little restrained by considerations of tradition. A central issue in the reformist movement was the ancient and powerful court known as the Areopagus, about which more will be said in connection with *The Eumenides*. The radicals proposed to strip this court of almost all the powers that it then held. The struggle over this was so fierce that one of Pericles' associates, Ephialtes, was assassinated in the course of it.

And all the while, during those years from 479 onward, a submerged force was beginning to operate in the life of Athens—a force at least as revolutionary as any of the postwar phenomena so far described. For the first time in history that we know of, a philosopher-scientist had taken up residence in the city.

For a century before that time, schools of philosophy-science (for the ancient Greeks those two activities were inseparable, both being understood under the term *philosophia*, "love of wisdom") had been arising in the outlying parts of the Greek-settled world: first in the cities of Ionia on the west coast of Asia Minor; somewhat later, in the colonies of Sicily and southern Italy. The individuals concerned were of very diverse outlooks and interests; their resistance, as a group, to classification is illustrated by the vague collective name for them that has become current in modern times, "the Pre-Socratics." Among them, however, by Aeschylus' last years, they had identified in one way or another many of the basic problems that still concern the modern philosopher and scientist, from epistemology to the nature of matter. Their proposed solutions to these problems, seen from a twentieth-century standpoint, were in some instances bizarre, in some astonishingly perceptive, in all too many reached with excessive haste in the then state of factual knowledge. Yet their glory was and remains that they had hit on the philosophic and scientific outlooks.

The Ionian school had been particularly interested in the question of how to explain the origin and composition of the universe on physical principles, without any recourse to the idea of divine intervention. It was in fact the last and perhaps the most sophisticated representative of that tradition, Anaxagoras, who was the first philosopher to arrive in Athens. He had been born in the Ionian city of Clazomenae—then, like all the cities of the region, ruled by Persia—and seems to have reached Athens in 480 B.C., possibly as one of the many Ionian conscripts who marched with the Persian horde. For the next several years—in some accounts as late as 450 B.C., after the death of Aeschylus—he stayed there. Most of his teaching was probably in oral form; we hear in particular of the long conversations he used to have with the democratic leader Pericles. He also, however, wrote a book, later known by the title of *Ta Physika*, "The Things of Nature." It is lost, but from the fragments and reports of its preserved in later

writers we can tell that it attempted a comprehensive account
of the universe, touching on cosmogony, astronomy, and bi-
ology, as well as the problems of knowledge and sensation.
At no point were gods invoked as an explanation of the phenomena. The nearest Anaxagoras came to anything of the
kind was in his hypothesis that *Nous*, "Mind," provided the
original motive force to stir the primal cloud of matter which
was to become the universe. "Mind," however, whatever exactly Anaxagoras meant by it, seems to have had nothing in
common with the traditional Greek hierarchy of gods.

Just how far Anaxagoras' thinking penetrated into Athenian society during his residence we cannot tell, but it had
certainly reached Pericles and, presumably, Pericles' circle;
there, at the core and center of the new democratic movement, the new philosophic-scientific learning was quietly at
work. Was Aeschylus aware of this thinking, the direct antithesis of the ancient mythic-religious thinking with which
he had grown up? Certainly he must have known Pericles
personally, since (as we shall see later) the two were associated in the production of *The Persians*. There is, further, evidence in the texts of his plays that seems to prove his
acquaintance with the new learning in general, and in some
cases in the form in which it was taught by Anaxagoras. In
The Suppliants 559, and again in a fragment of a lost play
(S 161), Aeschylus explains that ancient mystery, the summer
rising of the Nile, as due to the melting of the snows on the
African mountains far to the south of the known world. That
was precisely the explanation given by Anaxagoras; how close
it came to the truth was not to be recognized until the great
journeys of discovery in the Victorian age. Again, in Aeschylus' *Eumenides* 658–61, Apollo propounds a theory about the
process of human conception that was probably held by An-

axagoras, among other contemporary Pre-Socratics (see below, pp. 148–49).

The nature and the scale of the transition which took place during Aeschylus' middle and old age should by now be clear; as should the resultant tensions and dilemmas. In almost every area of human experience—religious, artistic, social, economic, and political—the immemorially old was being abruptly confronted by the utterly new. Aeschylus had been born into a culture, a religion, and a poetic tradition that had descended without any absolute break from the Bronze Age. Thereafter, and particularly after the defeat of Xerxes' invasion, he witnessed the beginnings of the modern world. It may not be too fanciful to compare the experience of Aeschylus and his contemporary Athenians with that of the citizen of any so-called developing nation in our own era. The crisis, both in the society concerned and in the individual psyche, may well have been similar. Where the parallel breaks down, of course, is in this: among the early fifth-century Greeks the sudden impetus toward a new way of life and thought sprang not from abroad but from within themselves. In this doubleness, within themselves and their society, was the very stuff of drama. In Aeschylus' extant plays, above all in the later ones, it is in fact realized in drama—the earliest drama that the West has known and, once understood, not the least powerful.

Aeschylus in the Period of the Extant Plays, 472–456 B.C.

Against that background we may now survey what is known specifically about Aeschylus' career during the last sixteen years of his life. The most certain information, as always, derives from the records of the tragic performances at the Great Dionysia, which are included in the Table of Dates at the end of this book.

In the spring of 472, Aeschylus produced the first of the seven plays of his that are extant, *The Persians*. The character of that performance will be discussed later; in the present biographical context it is noteworthy for two reasons. The first is that the name of the *choregos* (the citizen who trained and equipped the chorus at his own expense) on this occasion is recorded in an inscription: it is Pericles. This is positive evidence that Aeschylus must have become acquainted with the great democratic statesman almost a decade before the period of his constitutional reforms. The second is that, for whatever reason (its theme, the triumph of Greece over her invaders? or some novel quality in its art?), *The Persians* was a resounding success. Not only was it awarded the first prize at its original performance in Athens, but also Aeschylus was invited by Hieron, the famous ruler of Syracuse, to restage it in that city. His consequent visit to Sicily took place between the spring of 472 and the spring of 468, and may have been a fairly lengthy one; the rehearsal and production of so demanding an operatic and balletic work as an Aeschylean drama, especially in the alien conditions of the Syracusan court, would require a good deal of time in itself. We also know that in Sicily he composed and produced a new drama, *Aitnaiai*, "Women of Etna," as part of the inauguration ceremonies for the city of Aitna, which Hieron had recently founded close under the great volcanic mountain. That production most probably took place in the course of the same visit, although it is not impossible that he made a separate voyage for the purpose. In any case, it seems certain that during the late seventies or early sixties of the fifth century Aeschylus spent long enough in Sicily to become well acquainted with conditions there. Sicily, ever an island of wonders and extremes, has perhaps never been more so than in the years (478 to about 466 B.C.) when Hieron was lord of Syracuse. Even more strikingly than in contemporary Athens, one could meet side by side the very old and the very new. At Hieron's court were to be found, for example, the Ionian philosopher Xenophanes, the extraordinarily sophisticated comic dramatist Epicharmus, and many a visiting poet from Old Greece—Aeschylus' fellow tragedian Phrynichus, the great choral lyric poet Simonides, possibly even Pindar himself. Yet here and elsewhere on the island one might also meet many an Orphic-Pythagorean mystic, or the young aristocrat Empedocles, who improbably combined in one person the roles of medicine man, mystic, and scientist seriously in search of the material composition of the universe, and who expressed himself magnificently on all these matters in the ancient medium of hexameter poetry. As poet, as playwright, and perhaps not least as observer of the social and cultural scene, Aeschylus may well have been enthralled by what he saw and heard during his stay in Sicily, and by its implications for the future.

However that may be, he had returned to Athens in time to compete in the Dionysiac festival of spring 468 B.C., for we know that on that occasion he was defeated by Sophocles, then aged about twenty-eight and competing for the first time. This unhappy confrontation with the dramatist of the future—the dramatist who was to become the pace-setter for the tragedians of Greece and Europe over so many centuries—does not, however, seem to have meant more than a temporary setback. Aeschylus' career in the Athenian theater for the decade following it may be read from the Table of Dates. This decade saw the productions, each time victorious, of five of his seven extant plays: *The Seven Against Thebes* in 467, *The Suppliants* probably in 463, *Agamemnon, The Libation-*

Bearers, and *The Eumenides* in 458 (the Table of Dates, again, may be consulted for the *lost* plays associated with each of these productions). *Prometheus Bound,* which has come down to us without any external indication of its production date, is assumed in this book (on stylistic grounds) to have been composed very late in Aeschylus' life, perhaps concurrently with the *Oresteia* or even after it. That seems the likeliest assumption on the perplexing evidence that we have, but the reader should note that there are great differences of opinion about the dating of the *Prometheus,* and even about its authenticity (see further, in the Epilogue).

Aeschylus' last years and death are clouded in fable, but the following facts seem reasonably certain. Soon after the triumphant production of spring 458, he left Athens on another voyage to Sicily; and about two years later he died at Gela, a city on the southern coast of the island. On his tomb there, say a number of later Greek authors, one might read this inscription:

> This monument in wheatbearing Gela hides an Athenian
> dead: Aeschylus, son of Euphorion. Of his noble courage
> the sacred field of Marathon could tell, and the long-
> haired Mede, who had good cause to know.

The Greek original of that epitaph is in verse, but its simplicity and dignity are most easily conveyed in English through prose. There is no mention of Aeschylus' lifework as poet and playwright. The tomb says only that he was an Athenian who long before had played his part in what would forever be his city's most glorious military achievement—and that he died far from home.

The period of Aeschylus' extant plays saw an amazing outburst of artistic energy. Even on the surviving record, reproduced in the Table of Dates, we still have the names of twenty-four plays composed by him between 472 and his death. To these can be added the four plays (not named in the record) which lost to Sophocles' first production in 468; and also, though less certainly, the four (or even sixteen) plays implied in a statement by a late Greek author to the effect that one of Aeschylus' two sons, Euphorion II, "won four victories with works by his father Aeschylus, which the latter had not yet exhibited." This would suggest that by the time his life was cut short in Gela, Aeschylus had accumulated a number of plays designed for production in Athens on his return. On this evidence, Aeschylus' work as a playwright seems considerably to have intensified from his late middle age into his last years. It may not be coincidental that this same period saw both his visits to the brave new world of Sicily and the culmination in Athens of the great transition described earlier in the present chapter.

III THE POET
IN HIS THEATER

The Early Athenian Theater

THE ANCIENT GREEK WORDS *THEATRON, DRAMA, TRAGOIDIA, komoidia*, still in use with little or no modification in many of the major languages of the world, are a vivid reminder of the priority of the Greeks in this artistic sphere. Yet these words, and perhaps even more their related adjectives, *theatrical, dramatic, tragic, comic*, may also prove to be formidable obstacles to our enjoyment of the marvelous freedom of Aeschylus' art. How many of us, in our innocence, have first approached the plays of Aeschylus or of the other fifth-century Greek playwrights with an idea of the theater that ultimately derives from the Restoration playhouses? Or with an idea of tragedy received at hundredth hand from the theorizing, rarely more than half understood at best, of a great man who wrote many decades after classical tragedy had reached its fullest development, Aristotle? What we are actually approaching, in the study of Aeschylus, is a "theater," a "drama," and a "tragedy" that are not yet in being as we have known them since, but in becoming. It is probably best to watch and hear, in the first instance, as we might watch and hear today's unnamed performance in the middle of an inner-city park, without trying to categorize it until the end.

And, in fact, so far as can be told, the physical conditions in which an early Attic tragedy was enacted were rather more like those of a show in an inner-city park than those of a show on Broadway, for instance. The indispensable necessities for a performance were: daylight; a great crowd of watching citizens, of all conditions; and a level open space to contain whatever kind of show was to be put on. Not very much more than that is known with scientific precision about the Athenian theater of Aeschylus' time. The stone theater which the visitor admires today on the southeast slope of the Acropolis dates from more than a century after his death (and has also undergone drastic modifications, extending into Roman times), and the same is true of the other reasonably well-preserved stone theaters to be seen in Greece, including the famous example at Epidaurus. It is, indeed, assumed, and with considerable probability, that the early theater in which Aeschylus performed consisted already of the three major components of those extant theaters—*orchēstra*, auditorium and *skēnē*—but they must have been made of less enduring materials and less elaborate.

The first component, the *orchēstra* ("dance-place"), was simply a circular level space. The second, the auditorium, consisted of seats rising up from the *orchēstra* in concentric tiers and resting mostly on the natural rock of a hollow in the Acropolis slope. Two remarkable features of the auditoria in the extant stone theaters were: they embraced about two-thirds of the circumference of the *orchēstra*; and the geometric center of the curving seats was identical with the center of the *orchēstra*, with the result that any spectator on taking his seat would automatically face that center. Both features, of course, suggest that even in the relatively late stage of development represented by the extant theaters, the *orchēstra* was felt to be the most important component of the whole complex and the focal point of the performances. It seems reasonable to suppose that the same held true of the Aeschylean theater. The third component, the *skēnē*, is the most problematic. In the extant stone theaters it appears as a long rectangular building with slightly projecting wings at each end; it lies at a tangent to the *orchēstra*, almost filling the space between the inner corners of the auditorium but leaving room for entrance passages (called *parodoi*; sing. *parodos*) between itself and the auditorium on either side. Clearly its *orchēstra*-facing facade, pierced for doors, must have served to represent the houses, palaces, temples, or caves which are the backgrounds implied in the texts of most Greek tragedies and comedies. What the *skēnē* looked like in Aeschylus' day, however, is anybody's guess. It was no doubt made of perishable materials such as wood and canvas, as its very name suggests in Greek (the word means "tent" or "shack," a far cry indeed from the meanings of its modern derivatives, "scene" and "scenery"). Its presence seems absolutely required by the text of the *Oresteia*, where characters must frequently enter and exit through a back-scene which represents either a palace or (in *The Eumenides*) a temple, and where at least one character speaks from the palace roof; the text of *The Persians* implies but does not absolutely require a *skēnē*; the texts of the remaining extant plays offer no evidence about it one way or the other.

It may be added, finally, that all the extant plays of Aeschylus imply the existence in his day of the entrance passages or *parodoi* mentioned above; through these both the choruses and the actors (other than the denizens of the background buildings in the *Oresteia*) must regularly have entered and left the *orchēstra*, which was no doubt the focus of the performance.

The Early Tragic Medium

Such was the physical space within which an Aeschylean performance unfolded. The character of the performance itself can be grasped most simply through a consideration of his earliest surviving tragedy, *The Persians.* Here I shall reenact in brief its first three hundred lines.

For the purposes of this particular happening, two temporary additions, at most, are needed in the theatral area: a bench or step, presumably along the base of the *skēnē* (which, as lines 140–41 suggest, is here to be imagined as an ancient building in the Persian capital); and a structure, possibly in the middle of the *orchēstra*, representing the tomb of the late king, Darius. Suddenly that still setting becomes alive with movement, color, and sound, as the Chorus marches in through one of the entrance passages. At this date, probably, there are twelve chorus members, all of them masked and richly costumed to represent aged Persian nobles. They circle the *orchēstra* chanting in an anapestic march rhythm to the accompaniment of the *aulos*, a reed instrument whose nearest modern equivalent is the oboe. This majestic parade continues for three or four minutes. Then (line 65) the brilliant figures move into a rectangular formation, halt, and launch into full song, accompanied, it may be, by both the *aulos* and the lyre. The rhythm and sense of their song are reinforced and interpreted by dance, but the dance is of a kind in which body posture and hand gesture predominate. (Foot movements mattered less in the ancient dancing than in the modern; anyone who knows something of classical Greek sculpture, with its rhythmic, expressive postures, can gain some idea of this dancing from a remark by the Alexandrian scholar Athenaeus that the classical statues of the Greeks reflected their dance postures.) This song-dance runs for about five minutes; then (line 140) the Chorus breaks its rectangular formation and files toward the bench at the base of the *skēnē*, now chanting in the same march rhythm to which it first entered. They are about to take their seats in council when they are interrupted by the appearance of a resplendent figure, masked and cos-

tumed as the Queen Mother of the Persian realm, widow of
the great Darius. She comes into view probably through the
entrance passage opposite to that through which the Chorus
entered; she is borne onward with much pomp, in a magnificent chariot (for this, see her later reference in lines 607–08);
and all analogy in tragic practice suggests that so great a per-
sonage must be accompanied by a large procession of supernumeraries, masked and costumed as guards and attendant
ladies. The Chorus, overwhelmed, prostrates itself in a salaam, still chanting. Only at line 155 does it regain enough
composure to speak to her directly. At that point, for the first
time in *The Persians* and consequently for the first time in the
history of the West, we can hear dramatic lines that are neither chanted nor sung but spoken without accompaniment,
like the verse of Shakespeare or Racine.

Five lines later occurs another solemn moment in dramatic history: the actor playing the Queen responds to the
Chorus's greeting, again in spoken verse. A dialogue in that
medium develops, continuing until the arrival in great haste,
through one of the entrance passages, of an actor masked and
costumed as a Persian courier (line 246). At once, again in
spoken verse, he breaks the news that he bears. It is such
that the Chorus for its part can only express its reaction in
song and dance (lines 256–89, passim); the dance, which
would have mattered much at this point, is of course lost, but
the Greek words and their rhythms in themselves convey
chaos and despair. After that outburst the dialogue reverts to
the level of spoken verse and remains there for the rest of the
long scene (until line 531). For our present purpose we need
only pause to note one further landmark in dramatic history.
Up to now, even such dialogue as has occurred in *The Persians*
has been between an actor and a chorus, but from line 294
onward the actor masked as a queen enters into dialogue with

the actor masked as a courier. Here at last—more than a quarter of the way through the entire length of *The Persians*—we have reached the first passage where one individual discourses with another; the first passage, in fact, that can qualify as *drama* in the most basic sense in which drama has been understood for the last two thousand years and more.

This account of the early part of *The Persians* should be enough to give a fairly clear picture of the peculiar medium in which Aeschylus worked. He had at his disposal a chorus; two actors to perform speaking roles (by changing masks and costumes offstage, however—presumably behind the *skēnē*— each of them could impersonate several characters in the course of a play); and an indefinite number of silent supernumeraries. The entire cast was male, as on the Elizabethan stage; female roles, which were many, were achieved by a change of mask and costume and, we may guess, a variation in the pitch of the voice. He further had at his disposal three modes of vocal performance, which he could interweave at will to match the emotional level of any given passage in his play. In ascending degrees of intensity, these were: unaccompanied spoken verse, oboe-accompanied anapestic chant, and finally, full song, which was accompanied by oboe or lyre or both and was often given added expressiveness through the dance. Near the very end of Aeschylus' career, the number of actors available rose to three (the texts of the *Oresteia* and of the *Prometheus* both require this number for performance), and it may be that the number of the chorus was increased from twelve to fifteen.

In Aeschylus' time the poet-playwright was responsible for almost every aspect of the performance that he created out of these materials. His tragedies, as few dramatic works have ever been since, were from one end to the other the product of a single controlling brain and imagination. Aeschylus himself is known to have composed the music and devised the choreography. He himself was one of the two (or, later, three) actors. He himself "taught" his entire creation to the rest of the company (it is significant that the standard Greek word for the poet in his capacity of playwright is *didaskalos*, "teacher") and oversaw its production. The only limit set to his artistic autonomy was financial: the provision of properties, masks, and costumes was the province of the *choregos* assigned by the state to each poet at any given festival. The generosity or stinginess of this official thus might considerably affect the external trappings of a performance; but its essential quality, in concept and in execution, was entirely the responsibility of Aeschylus.

I have reserved until last the most awesome of all Aeschylus' responsibilities, the poetry itself. Too many modern translations into English, successful as they are in bringing across this aspect of his plays or that, obscure the fact that an Aeschylean tragedy is a complex and exquisitely composed verbal poem, moving easily at will through an enormous range of rhythms and tones. It is not easy to think of any *single* English poem, by however great a master, that offers a really close analogy to the poetry of any Attic tragedian in this respect, but perhaps Aeschylus is the hardest to parallel of them all. Nearest, perhaps, comes Milton's *Samson Agonistes*, a deliberate attempt to match the effects of Greek tragedy. Even that does not come very close, for the English language, even in Milton's hands, is by nature incapable of the precision and variety of Greek's metrical effects. Further, I myself feel a strained solemnity throughout Milton's play that is not really characteristic of Greek tragedy. Rather, one would have to seek analogies here and there in a dozen English poets to this or that aspect of Aeschylean poetry. Aeschylus' compact and loaded phrases may sometimes recall

Donne; his sonorous iambic versification, Marlowe; in his choral poetry the fascinating rhythms as well as the rich compound words often remind one of Hopkins. There are a few marvelous moments when the singing has a simplicity and immediacy that approach those of Shakespeare's dramatic lyrics. We are, in short, dealing with a consummate poetic craftsman here, even if we abstract his verbal poetry from all the other elements of his dramaturgy that were described above, and simply judge it against the work of later poets who composed for reading, not staging; even if we are prepared temporarily to forget that his poetry was in fact a harmony of words, music, dance, mask, and costume—in its own way as complex and as integrated as an orchestral symphony.

At the same time, as the above sketch of the early scenes of *The Persians* may have demonstrated, the verbal poetry dominated an Aeschylean performance to an extent unparalleled in any later drama. There were long passages in which the verbal poetry carried the entire weight, in which the audience had absolutely nothing to occupy its attention except the words issuing from the mouths of masks. There were not even the changing facial expressions of an actor to engage the eye; the effects achieved this way by the modern actor (so important an element in his art and our enjoyment of it) had to be achieved predominantly by the Greek actor's *voice*. Further, as we saw, a long stretch of *The Persians* goes by before any actor appears at all, and still another long stretch before he is joined by a second one. In each case, the sudden intrusion of a new corporeal entity is a major event in itself. Aeschylean "entrances" are never to be received casually: "epiphanies" might be a better description of them, epiphanies not simply of characters but also of ideas and moral forces. Like many other Aeschylean visual effects—such as the tapestry tableau of the *Agamemnon*, to be discussed later—they

usually mark high and significant points in the elaborate au-
dio-visual fabric that is an Aeschylean tragedy. They prolong
into another dimension, and may often bring to consumma-
tion, the effects gradually created by the verbal poetry, the
music, and the dance.

Tragedy before Aeschylus

At this point one may well be inclined to ask how such
an extraordinary kind of performance as that described in the
preceding section could ever have come into existence. There
survive a few fairly well ascertained facts about tragedy before
the time of Aeschylus; and although they do not add up to
anything approaching a continuous history of the early stages
of the art, they seem worth stating here. They at least allow
us to set Aeschylus' career as a playwright in some sort of
historical perspective, and to appreciate the immensity of his
creative achievement.

In 534 B.C., or a year very close to that, a contest in tragic
performances was established as part of the Athenians' spring
festival held in honor of the god Dionysus, the Great Dionysia. That date is as far back as we can go with any certainty
in the story of tragedy. Common sense alone would suggest
that it had been practiced in some form or other long before
the official institution of the contests. Neither common sense,
however, nor the abundant ancient and modern speculations
avail to reconstruct the nature of the art in the years before
534; still less, to account for the extraordinary name by which
its practitioners were known—*tragoidoi*, "goat-singers," from
which was fairly soon derived the name of the art itself, *tragoidia*, "goat-song." From 534 onward, however, there at least
survive the names of a few tragic poets, beginning with that
of Thespis, who performed at the first contest and won the

prize; then, as Aeschylus' time nears, not merely names but even a few scraps of the pioneer tragic poetry are transmitted. From reports in later classical sources it appears that for the first thirty or forty years of the official contests the tragedies were performed by a chorus and a single actor. This in itself might suggest that the pre-Aeschylean tragedies relied even more heavily than did those of Aeschylus on choral singing and dancing, less on spoken dialogue. If we can trust the comic poet Aristophanes, even the plays of Aeschylus' immediate predecessor in the succession of tragedians, Phrynichus, were remembered above all for their songs. In his *The Wasps* (lines 219–20) Aristophanes describes how, as late as the 420s B.C., aged Athenians might still be heard humming Phrynichus' "honey-sweet-sexy-Sidonian songs" in the street—one of many Greek references, incidentally, that show how the poetry of tragedy, like the hits of a modern musical, was apt to escape from the confines of the theater into the ordinary life of the city.

Aeschylus brought about certain changes that were clearly crucial. "He diminished the part of the chorus," says Aristotle in the fourth chapter of his *Poetics*, "and he gave the leading role to [unaccompanied] speech." Furthermore, at some time between his first performance in ca. 498 B.C. and his production of *The Persians* in 472, he introduced the employment of a second actor in the tragedies. A dialogue onstage between two individuals could and did now take place (for the first surviving instance of this, see above). From the moment of that innovation we may fairly date the origin—although by no means, as yet, the full realization—of Western drama as we know it. That exotic kind of performance which the sixth-century Athenians nicknamed *tragoidia* might have taken some very different course, for all we can tell. That it was, in fact, pointed along the road toward drama seems to have been due to the genius of Aeschylus.

PART II
THE POETIC DRAMAS

IV THE POETRY OF THE FRAGMENTARY PLAYS

O<small>NLY THOSE LOST PLAYS OF AESCHYLUS THAT ARE KNOWN TO</small> have been produced on the same occasions as the surviving seven (see the Table of Dates) can be dated with some certainty. Statistically it is likely that many of the remainder, between fifty and sixty in number, were composed during the long period extending from Aeschylus' first performance in ca. 498 B.C. to the production of *The Persians* in 472. Some of the fragments to be quoted in this chapter, therefore, may, for all we know, take us back to the time of his earliest experiments with the art of *tragoidia*. The fragments taken as a whole without reference to chronology, however, will perhaps provide our best approach to certain fundamental characteristics of his imagination and his art.

Mere fragments, obviously, can reveal little or nothing of the architectonics of our poet's dramaturgy, or of the profound religious and moral issues that he was capable of developing even out of the most exotic legends in the course of a play. Those larger questions await the chapters on his extant works. Yet a first confrontation with one of the surviving plays can be so overwhelming that one may actually fail to take in many of the features that are the subject of this chapter. For instance, as one gazes down the vistas that open up below the surface of *Agamemnon* (vistas as terrifying as one's first glimpse, in childhood, into a pair of opposite mirrors), one may be apt to lose sight of the poetic texture itself. Aeschylus can create an electrifying miniature poem out of a pair of words; and his sympathy with the entire world of archaic myth is such that he can bring any detail of it, however bizarre, to credible life, with pathos or humor or a surreal imagination. The fragments of the lost plays—a casual anthology put together by Time—can introduce us, indeed, only to the surface of his art. But what a surface!

We may begin from a few fragments that consist, in the original Greek, of two to six words—fragments in the absolutely literal sense, tiny splinters broken off from what once were complete plays, now deprived of any context. Aeschylus, we are told, somewhere described smoke as "spindrift of fire" (M 658). The death-god, Hades, he once riddlingly called "Lord of the Host" (M 612). In another fragment (S 93), someone, evidently mentally or physically sick, "through his lungs heaves hot sleep"; and yet another reads "life's sentry-watch is over" (M 249). Such allusive and endlessly evocative language is characteristic of all the plays, fragmentary and extant; since not all our translations seek to bring it out, a few literal versions from the latter group also may be worth contemplating here:

> Most reverend of the stars, Night's glaring eye
> > [*Seven Against Thebes* 390: the full moon]

> A lonely-thinking rock beyond our pointing
> > [*Suppliants* 795: a mountain peak]

> A mighty beard of flame
> > [*Agamemnon* 306: a beacon-fire]

> Her ashes spurt rich airs of wealth
> > [*Agamemnon* 820: the ruins of Troy]

Night shall screen day with her star-embroidered cloak
[*Prometheus* 24]

It is easy, of course, for a modern reader to docket such
phrases as simple instances of metaphor and file them away.
But with Aeschylus, it seems (as with some of his great contemporary poets, above all Pindar), we are still in a time before grammatical analysis is thinkable, before the intellectual
chasm between signifier and signified has opened up. A
word, for him, seems still to be a *vision.* And in fact the uni-
tary mode of seeing and feeling casually revealed in these
little word-groups appears at all levels of Aeschylus' art. Apparently separate phenomena, for him, pass into each other
and illuminate each other. This is the mode of vision that
allowed Leonardo da Vinci, for instance, to compare (in words
and drawings) the fall of a cascade to the flow of a woman's
hair—and to deepen our comprehension of both.

Some longer quotations that have survived from the lost
plays may serve to illustrate the great range of Aeschylus'
sensibility. Too long has the idea prevailed that Attic tragedy
is a preternaturally solemn art, and that the earlier the tragedian, the more solemn he must be—and the more tense
and straight-faced his audiences and readers. Aeschylean
tragedy in fact almost approaches Shakespearean tragedy in
its ability to play the diapason of human feelings, to put into
perspective the meaning not just of suffering but of all life.
The following fragments are arranged in descending order of
seriousness. In the first of them Aeschylus formulates, as
starkly as perhaps no one but an ancient Greek would have
dared to do, an inescapable condition of our existence:

For Death, alone
Of all the Gods, yearns not for gifts. You may not

Win him by sacrifice or by libation.
Death seeks no altars, and no hymns of praise.
From him alone of all the immortal spirits
Persuasion stands aloof.

[S 82]

The house is god-filled and the roof is reveling.

[S 28; from a Dionysiac play, the *Edonoi*]

We, honoring
Kotȳtō's rites, one holding
The oboes, labor of the lathe,
Breathing a tune with tapping fingers,
In notes that charm to madness;
Another clashing brass-bound cymbals . . .
And the twanging strings resound,
Bull-voices bellowing from the unseen;
Crash of tambours, terror-filled,
Echoes like thunder under ground.

[S 27, also from the *Edonoi*:
an orgiastic rite for a Thracian goddess]

This, this is he
Who slung the funniest of missiles at me—
A stinking chamber-pot! He did not miss:
Around my head it shipwrecked into sherds,
Breathing aromas different far from myrrh!

[S 95; Odysseus describes his treatment
at the hands of the Suitors]

I shall not fail to mark
The glowing eye of a girl who has tasted man,
For in these things I am a connoisseur. . . .

[S 134]

The range of subject matter in Aeschylus' work as a whole was just as striking as its range of tone. Certain regions of the vast and ancient mythological world which his imagination inhabited are still fairly familiar to a modern reader, for since Aeschylus' time they have been repeatedly traversed by the dramatists of the West from Sophocles to Edward Bond. Thebes, Argos, Mycenae, and Troy, for instance, with all the horrors that they witnessed long ago, are still part of our imaginative geography. As far as our information goes, it was in fact Aeschylus who set the precedent for dramatizing the adventures of the heroes who were associated with those ancient sites; it is to him that we seem to owe the canonical themes of all subsequent Attic tragedy, as they still appear in Milton's famous couplet:

Presenting *Thebes*, or *Pelops* line
Or the tale of *Troy* divine.

No such themes are traceable in the fragments of the pre-Aeschylean tragedians. Among Aeschylus' lost plays, however, we can make out an *Oedipus*, an *Iphigenia*, a *Philoctetes*, and several tragedies based on the stories of Ajax and Odysseus; while his extant work, of course, includes treatments of the fates of Agamemnon, the matricide Orestes, and the fratricidal sons of Oedipus.

Yet such now familiar heroic themes occupied scarcely a quarter of Aeschylus' dramatic output as it originally stood. The titles and fragments of the remaining three-quarters open up a wild mythological landscape that seems to be bounded by no horizons of space, time, or credibility—a very ancient landscape, which few later European dramatists, or even Attic dramatists, were ever to explore again on the stage. For any glimpses of it elsewhere than in Aeschylus we have to turn not to the drama but rather to the vase-painters and sculptors of Aeschylus' youth and of the two or three generations before him, and to certain great poets of the archaic period, notably Hesiod and Pindar. It is a landscape rich in magic—the kind of magic which, long afterward, Antonin Artaud desiderated for his ideal theater. Here is a brief survey of those tracts of it that can be glimpsed through the plays and fragments of Aeschylus.

Not merely Thebes and the plains of Argos and Troy but the entire eastern Mediterranean area, seen through these eyes, are thickly populated with legendary heroes and heroines. Many of them no doubt perpetuated the memory of dynasts, Minoan or Mycenaean, who had once lived and ruled in the various cities and islands concerned before the collapse of the Bronze Age civilizations; others have the air of faded gods. To take the Greek mainland first: in Corinth we find the tricky Sisyphus, who once outwitted Death himself (Aeschylus composed two plays entitled *Sisyphus*); in Boeotia, the maniacal Athamas (commemorated in a tragedy of the same name), husband first to a woman named Nephele, "Cloud," then to one named Leucothea, "White-Goddess"; in the Arcadian mountains, the fair Callisto (treated in the play *Callisto*), who hunted the wild creatures there before Zeus fell in love with her and transformed her into a bear. The feats of the great female athlete Atalanta (treated in the like-named play) ranged from Arcadia to Thessaly. In the latter region once ruled Ixion, who committed the first of all murders within a family, was purified by Zeus, and rewarded this grace by trying to rape Hera (some, at least, of the incidents in this strange story were dramatized in the *Ixion*). Beyond the Greek mainland in almost all directions dwelled legendary beings whose characters and actions were no less strange. The *Women of Etna*, set far away in Sicily, included the local story of a nymph, Thalia, who was impregnated by Zeus and entrusted the resulting twin embryos to Earth, from whose depths they eventually emerged as gods, under the name Palikoi, "The Returners." Traveling southward from Greece through this Aeschylean world, we should come first to Crete, where, in the *The Carians* (alternatively entitled *Europa*) and *The Cretan Women*, were enacted the very ancient legends that centered on the great sea-king Minos. Further south still lay the settings of *The Proteus* (the name of the Old Man of the Sea whom Menelaus encountered on an island off the Egyptian coast) and of the *Phorkides*; the heroines of the latter are better known as the Graeae, the three ancient hags with only one eye between them, who lived in the Libyan desert and were outwitted by Perseus during his journey in quest of Medusa's head.

But it was to the northeast of Greece proper that some of the greatest wonders were found. The mountainous coast of Thrace was preeminently the domain of Dionysus and his wild worshipers, and Aeschylus devoted an entire tetralogy, *The Lykourgeia*, to the story of the Thracian king Lycurgus, who there opposed the god and his rites. One of the plays of that group, the *Bassarides*, also introduced the fate of Orpheus, the greatest of all legendary singers. Aeschylus' treatment of this story is recorded in some detail: instead of honoring the newly arrived Dionysus, Orpheus held to his belief that the Sun was the greatest of all the gods and would adore him each day at dawn from the heights of Mount Pangaios. For this the local Bacchantes tore him to pieces; but in the end his patron goddesses, the Muses, collected his remains and gave them burial among the mountains of Macedonia (M 85). Standing out from that cruel coast toward the Hellespont, we should pass between the isles of Samothrace and Lemnos. In this area Aeschylus set a group of plays, *Lemnian Women, Hypsipyle, Kabeiroi,* and *Argo* (possibly forming a connected tetralogy), on the wondrous adventures of

Jason and the Argonauts. Lemnos was also the scene of Aeschylus' *Philoctetes*, which in its general theme anticipated the famous extant play by Sophocles but showed (said a later Greek critic who was lucky enough to read a text of it still intact) "the grandeur of Aeschylus' spirit and his antique dignity; the sternness of its ideas and diction seemed to me appropriate to tragedy as well as to the character of the heroes of old, for there was nothing there contrived, no idle talk for talk's sake, nothing base" (M 394). Next, opening the narrows of the Hellespont and leaving to starboard the ruins of Troy, richest of all sites in heroic memories, we should at last emerge into the Euxine, the Black Sea.

Northward along the coastline lay Salmydessos, where once Phineus, king and seer, contended with the Harpies; those loathsome monsters, birds of prey with women's faces, perpetually swooped down and befouled his food, and he was close to starvation until the Sons of the North Wind arrived aboard Jason's ship the *Argo*, and slew them (this story was told in the *Phineus*, produced along with the extant *Persians* in 472 B.C.). Farther northward yet, and eastward, beyond the treacherous waters of the Euxine, the Aeschylean world-map shows a region of pure marvel. There lie the Russian steppes, roamed by the Scythian hordes, among them the Gabioi, "the justest people of all" (S 110); passing beyond them over the icy mountains, one would come in time to the blessed Hyperboreans, "the people above the North Wind," who dwell in eternal peace. At the eastern end of the Euxine towers the Caucasus, a massif of unknown extent; somewhere among those airy peaks Prometheus was savagely punished by the eagle of Zeus in the lost *Prometheus Unbound*. That tragedy and its extant companion piece, *Prometheus Bound*, in the prophetic speeches to Herakles and Io respectively, provided between them a survey of the entire fantasized world that lay beyond the lands known to the Greek navigators of Aeschylus' time, from central Asia westward to the Pillars of Herakles that guard the Straits of Gibraltar, and southward into the burning sands of Africa and the cataracts of the Nile. The denizens of these areas may well call to mind the monsters that writhe in the margins of the maps drawn in the great age of European oceanic exploration. Indeed, many are identical with those found on the Renaissance maps, since to a great extent they are creatures of international and timeless fantasy: the one-eyed Arimaspian race of *Prometheus Bound* 804–05, for instance; or the Dog-Heads and Chest-Eyes, whom Aeschylus mentioned in some now unidentifiable play or plays (M 603, 604).

Such are the bare outlines of the imaginative world that was available to Aeschylus in all its fullness; and not to him only, but to all the Greeks of his generation. It was a *shared* imaginative world—in some sense, even a shared subconscious—which contained not only almost every imaginable pattern of human behavior but also almost every imaginable dream, every level of fantasy. Yet in evaluating Aeschylean drama we should never for one moment forget that the Greeks did not live out their lives merely in that rich dreamworld of their myths. Simultaneously they lived, and with a passionate intensity almost unimaginable to modern urban man, in this dirty world that all we human beings know at all eras, this world of sex, economics, politics, and war. The singularity of archaic and classical Greek art in any medium, visual or verbal, is that it applies that dreamworld to the interpretation of our own world: in order to make some sense of our actual workaday lives, it resorts to the universally shared inheritance of myth. This strange tension between mythical imagination and down-to-earth reality appears in Attic tragedy more clearly than in any other kind of Greek art. But among the tragedians we feel it most, perhaps, in Aeschylus, a poet who both commanded a perfect knowledge of the age-old mythology and religion and, toward the end of his career, experienced an intellectual, political, and military revolution of world-historical importance. For a sympathetic understanding of the ways in which he reconciled these two diverse facets of his life experience, we clearly have to turn to those of his tragedies that survive complete. I hope that the snippets of Aeschylus' work that occupy this chapter may have prepared the reader to cope with his technique in detail, and with the purely imaginative side of his art—a side which might appeal to any professional poet from Milton, through Yeats, to Dylan Thomas—but we are hardly yet halfway to that art in its totality. For his art, like that of all the greatest Greek poets, addressed itself to life—*was* life.

Nonetheless, it seems worth while to conclude this survey with a few fragments and ancient testimonies that allow glimpses, not merely of Aeschylean myth or phraseology, but of the lost tragedies in action. They are, indeed, random glimpses, but complaints about this should be laid not at my door but at that of Time. For these fragments, like all the others, we depend on the whims either of ancient authors—for the most part grammarians and lexicographers—who happen to have quoted the lost plays for their own peculiar purposes, or of the climate of Egypt, where so many tattered papyri of our poet's dramas have come to light since the beginning of the present century.

What did the choreography of Aeschylus look like? A faint idea of the answer to this may be obtained from a passage in the late fifth-century comic poet Aristophanes (M 246):

> [*Unidentified speaker*:]   I know it!
> Watching the Phrygians, when they followed Priam,

    To ransom his dead son, I saw them turn
    Often this way, often that way, often hither, posturing!

Here we have a glimpse of the play called *Phrygians* or *The Ransoming of Hector*, which was probably the last in the trilogy that Aeschylus composed on the story told by Homer in Books 16–24 of the *Iliad*: the slaying of Achilles' dearest friend, Patroclus, by Hector; Achilles' reentry into battle to avenge him; his slaying of Hector; and the expedition of Hector's father, King Priam, to ransom the corpse from Achilles. In Aeschylus' dramatized version of that final episode, evidently, a chorus of Phrygians (i.e., Trojans) accompanied Priam across the lines to Achilles' lodge and there reinforced his supplications by vivid, statuesque dance-postures. One can almost see this coup de theatre; the emotional situation is almost pure Homer, but Aeschylus has transposed it from words into dance.

    Less Homeric is another episode probably from that same trilogy. In a speech—or speeches—in the first play (*The Myrmidons*), Achilles, crazy with grief, uttered this terrible lament over the body of his slain friend Patroclus:

    Honored you not the glory of our thighs—
    You ill-repayer of my many kisses?

                      [S 64]

    Also my reverent converse with your thighs . . .

                      [S 65]

    Yet—for I love him!—this does not revolt me.

                      [S 66]

Here is a carnally homosexual Achilles—a facet of the great hero unknown to Homer and yet, it may seem, not altogether inconsistent with the Achilles whom Homer depicts. Aeschy-

lus in his trilogy perhaps added the last, necessary psychological touch that might make sense of Achilles' actions in the
later books of the *Iliad*.

From the utterly tragic (for does not the impermanence
of human lives and loves lie at the core of tragedy?), we may
turn for relief to the ancient reports of one of Aeschylus' plays
about the Argonauts. The great gods named *Kabeiroi* presided
over a mystic cult that was honored above all in the isles of
Samothrace and Lemnos, and in the play named after them
Aeschylus introduced these deities as jestingly threatening
their worshipers:

> There'll be no vinegar in all your houses!
>
> [Fragment S 49]

—meaning, apparently, that the only drink available henceforth will be *wine*. Possibly to the same episode refers the
report (Fragment M 46) that "Aeschylus in the *Kabeiroi* brings
Jason and his company drunk onstage." Of course, there can
be no reconstructing such a fantastic scene in detail; yet we
may justifiably use it as one datum in our reconstruction of
the imagination of Aeschylus.

And here is yet another scene from the lost tragedies;
whether, in fact, we should label it tragedy or black comedy
or just sensuous poetry I shall leave to the reader's judgment.
In Aeschylus' *Thracian Women* (M 292) a Messenger announces
the suicide of Ajax. From this speech it appears that this great
hero, second only to Achilles in valor, was invulnerable in
every part of his body except the armpits; for long before,
Herakles had wrapped him in his famous lionskin to protect
him against all injuries, but the skin had not touched him in
these two spots. Hence, when Ajax eventually attempted suicide, "his sword bent against his body, which would nowhere
yield to the wounding. He strained it like a bow" (these six

words may well be the actual words of Aeschylus' play) "until some deity came to his side and showed him where he had to strike."

These are only a selection from the remains of Aeschylus' lost plays. The reader who wishes to explore them further would do well to look at the fragments of the so-called *Dike*-drama (S 282), of the *Glaukos of the Sea* (S 13–19 and 273), and of the *Psychostasia* or "Soul-weighing" (M 204–10), if no others.

But it is time to turn to yet another of the facets of Aeschylus' mind and art that are revealed in the fragments. Throughout the period of the extant Attic tragedies, each tragedian who competed at the Great Dionysia Festival produced a tetralogy, consisting of three tragedies followed by a satyr-play. Of all the performances that made up the total experience of the Athenian theatergoer, the satyr-play is the most remote from anything that we moderns have ever experienced. It is worth pausing to consider what its effects must have been like within the context of a complete Aeschylean production. The last of today's three tragedies has just ended. The stately heroes, heroines, and gods have left the *skēnē*, and the solemnly robed chorus has filed, singing or chanting, out of the *orchēstra*. At least if that final tragedy of the sequence has been a work of the quality of *The Seven Against Thebes*, for instance, or of *The Eumenides*, we are in shock; we are not the same people we were when we took our seats at the beginning of the trilogy. Suddenly the atmosphere of the theater is transformed. There is a gasp, then a ripple of smiles through the auditorium, as a dozen lithe dancers caper into the *orchēstra*, naked except for grotesque satyr-masks and short tights; these last have strange appendages, horse tails and mock phalluses. The dancing is wild (as we know from the many vase-paintings that show choruses of satyrs), including a number of exaggerated postures comparable to the Anglo-Saxon attitudes of Haigha in *Through the Looking-Glass*. An invariable member of the cast is the elderly Silenus, who is dressed in a body-suit covered with tufts of white hair. The nonsatyric members of the cast are—shockingly enough—heroes, heroines, and deities drawn from the regular tragic repertoire (often, indeed, these same characters will have appeared in the immediately preceding tragic trilogy). These latter are apt to be mocked, abused, cheated, and even sexually assaulted by the satyrs, who know no moral restraints of any kind, being forest-spirits, almost personifications of the untamed wilderness. The action is shorter than that of the average tragedy, and yet, at any rate in Aeschylus, the poetic craftsmanship seems not inferior to that of the tragedies.

The satyric mode was understandably not to the taste of later, and more solemn, generations of audiences and readers. Only a single Attic satyr-play, Euripides' *Cyclops*, survived the Middle Ages complete, and by a lucky accident at that. In the last century or so, however, fairly substantial papyrus fragments have come to light, including parts of Aeschylus' satyr-plays *Prometheus Pyrkaeus* ("Prometheus the Fire-Lighter"), *Theoroi or Isthmiastai* ("Pilgrims"; alternative title, "Satyrs at the Isthmian Games"), and *Diktyoulkoi* ("Satyrs Hauling on the Net"). These bear out the reports in later classical authors that Aeschylus was the most successful of all Attic playwrights in composing satyr-plays. They seem to have offered no less scope for his poetic genius than did the tragic mode; at the same time the satyr-play fragments reveal here and there a playful quality, a lightness of touch, of a kind that can scarcely be sensed in his extant tragedies. Here are a couple of examples.

Prometheus Pyrkaeus formed the finale of the tetralogy that included the extant *Persians* (again we may pause to wonder

at the range of tone and theme possible even within the limits
of a single Aeschylean production). Probably more than a decade later, as will be seen in chapter 7, Aeschylus was to
compose three solemn tragedies under the name of this ancient and mysterious deity, whose exploits and sufferings had
occurred so far back in the history of the mythic universe. In
the satyric play that we are now considering, however, the
poet landed this same god among the frisky satyrs. It had the
marvelous theme of the first appearance of fire on this earth.
Two glimpses of the action survive. One of the satyrs, apparently at his first sight ever of the fantastic loveliness of a
flame, is rushing to kiss it until Prometheus warns him,
"You'll be like the proverbial goat, in mourning for your
beard!" (S 117). In another fragment (S 278 = M 343), a per-
former who, I think, is probably Silenus, is singing and dancing around a bonfire; the refrain that punctuates his song may
perhaps be sung by the ensemble of satyrs. Although the
papyrus of the fragment is damaged and there are several
uncertainties about the detailed interpretation, its general
drift may be translated as follows:

> . . . The kindly gift
> Sets me to dancing:
> Round the unwearied glare of fire
> I swing my shining robe.
> A Fountain Nymph
> Shall hear my call
> And chase me, chase me round the glowing hearth!
>
> [REFRAIN:]
> *Nymphs of the Wild shall surely form their choirs*
> *In honor of Prometheus' gift,*
>
> Singing sweetly for the Giver:
> "Prometheus, for humanity

Life-bringer!
Showerer of gifts!"
So singing shall they dance,
Sure of protection from the winter's rage!

Nymphs of the Wild shall surely form their choirs
In honor of Prometheus' gift.

Shepherds too shall shine in dancing,
In the night-reel wandering,
Crowned with perfect
Leaves, on-springing . . .

The Goatfoot Gods shall surely in their caverns
Merrily drink beside the fire,

. . . .

V THE SEVEN EXTANT PLAYS: GENERAL CONSIDERATIONS

As WE TURN FROM THE SCATTERED BUILDING-BLOCKS AND HALF-effaced ground plans of Aeschylus' dramatic poetry to the seven monumental structures that survive complete, it is well first to recall the verses quoted at the opening of this book:

City and Earth and shining Water,
And Gods of highest heaven,
And Gods deep-honored under ground
Who hold the tombs,
And Zeus, third, Savior!

That vision never left Aeschylus—that sense of a *complete* universe, all of whose components relate to each other and affect each other, whether they are vast visible entities like Earth and Water, or great moral-religious powers, or even creatures like ourselves, now living, now dead. Yet Aeschylus' perception (which, as I should perhaps repeat, is in this book simply a short way of saying "the perception deducible from Aeschylus' plays") of the workings and nature of that universe seems to have changed profoundly during the period of the extant plays. From that point of view, those plays, for all their immense variety in theme, story-line, and technique, seem divisible into two groups. I myself do not think it in the least coincidental that the plays of the first group are earlier in date

than the plays of the second; that question, however, is ultimately for the reader to decide on the basis of the considerations to be presented.

In the first group, comprising *The Persians* and *The Seven
Against Thebes*, the cosmos remains an intact, static unity. If
man transgresses its laws, all the nonhuman powers will
swing into action to discipline him. No questions are allowed,
and no appeals. This cosmos of the first group has an im-
measurably ancient history behind it, and not only among the
Greek people; its basic character is such that most polytheists
of the ancient world, from Hittite Anatolia through Mesopo-
tamia as far as India, might have felt at home in it, if not at
ease. Of all surviving Greek documents, *The Persians* and *The
Seven Against Thebes* realize that ancient cosmos most powerfully. That is one element, although only one of many, in
their fascination. Through them we come about as close as is
still possible to entering the universe of preclassical man in
the Mediterranean and Middle Eastern areas. Indeed, some
analogies to the basic character of this universe, and to the
ways of life and thought that it implied, can be found even
farther afield than that—for example, among the Indians of
the American Southwest.

The second group comprises *The Suppliants, The Oresteia,*
and *Prometheus Bound.* In these productions—less certainly in
the first but with absolute and terrifying clarity in the others—
the ancient cosmos is riven asunder, and the ancient certainties are gone. In this group no one seems any longer to be
sure what the universal law is, and an apparent transgressor,
far from being annihilated by the combined powers of the
cosmos, may find those powers furiously divided over the
merits of his case. For a time, at least, both the divine and
the human worlds are split. In the only trilogy that survives
entire, the *Oresteia,* the rift is finally healed, and we end with

a universe united and at peace. But the ultimate harmony thus achieved is very different from the funereal harmony of the cosmos presupposed in the first group of the extant plays. In the *Oresteia* that fact is certain. In the final chapter I shall adduce some reasons for thinking that the trilogies containing *The Suppliants* and *Prometheus Bound*, respectively, may have followed a similar course overall, from discord to harmony. Even if we confine our observation to the nonfragmentary plays of these trilogies, however, it seems plain that they, like the *Oresteia*, introduce us to a world psychologically, morally, religiously, and politically different from the world of the first group.

What could have happened in the interval between the two groups—that is, between *The Seven Against Thebes* of 467 and *The Suppliants*, probably of 463—that might account for the change? Of course, no one can answer that with dogmatic assurance at this distance of time. Yet a glance at the Table of Dates will show that the overwhelmingly important event in Athenian history during the years from about 463 until the end of Aeschylus' residence in Athens was the violent struggle to replace the old constitution by the radical democracy—with all that entailed for the intellectual, as well as the political and social, life of the city. The momentous Periclean experiment lifted off on its great and ultimately tragic trajectory precisely during the years covered by the second group of Aeschylus' extant plays. Merely on chronological grounds, then, it would be difficult not to suspect a connection, and perhaps a very close one, between the two phenomena. But we shall see other and more positive grounds for that suspicion; most notably, the *Oresteia* (above all, in its last play, *The Eumenides*) is clearly engaged with the political upheaval of its time and contains many overt references to it. We may not be far wrong in viewing the plays of the second group as a commentary on the coming of a new world—*our* world? And yet, as was stressed in chapters 1 and 2, the mythic and religious language in which that commentary is expressed remains to the very end the language that Aeschylus—and, no doubt, the great majority of his contemporary Athenian audience— had inherited from untold generations past. That is the greatest obstacle to our modern understanding of it; that, also, its greatest fascination.

At this point a little more needs to be said about the Attic tragedian's practice of producing his dramas in groups of four, which was touched on at the end of the preceding chapter; with Aeschylus it involves some very important problems of interpretation. The practice persisted well into the fourth century B.C., but Aeschylus differed sharply from the later tragedians in that he seems often to have composed his tetralogy for any given competition *around a single mythological story.* Such "connected tetralogies," as they are called, consisted of three tragedies in sequence, each one having its own dramatic unity and yet combining with the others to form a single supertragedy, as it were, on the legend concerned, in such a way that the ultimate denouement was reserved for the end of the third play; these were followed by a satyr-play, which dramatized some farcical side of the same legend. All Aeschylus' extant plays with the exception of *The Persians* appear to have been units of connected tetralogies; in *The Persians* production (at least on most views) Aeschylus adopted what later became the regular practice, in that his tetralogy consisted of four independent plays, each on a discrete theme. The Table of Dates, in which the surviving units from each tetralogy are indicated by capital letters, will at once show the problem that results: in effect, we possess only two *complete* tragic compositions by Aeschylus, *The Persians* and the

Oresteia trilogy. Of the other extant plays, *The Seven Against Thebes* preserves only the *conclusion* of a sequence of three tragedies which traced the saga of a great Theban family over three generations; *The Suppliants* and *Prometheus Bound* are among the most difficult and most challenging of Greek tragedies for the interpreter, because each preserves only the ambiguous *opening* of its tragic trilogy—the tying of a complex knot in innumerable strands. In these broken trilogies we can to some extent infer the outlines of the missing plays from such of their fragments as survive, and from backward or forward allusions in the play that is extant. But this is obviously an uncertain business. One of the duties of a conscientious interpreter of Aeschylus, a role I shall attempt to fulfill in this book to the best of my ability, is to keep his reader informed at all stages as to what in his accounts of the missing plays is assured fact, and what is more or less probable inference.

Finally, a few words on the approach that I shall adopt to the discussion of the extant plays. The aim of this book, as of the Hermes series generally, is to guide the reader toward his or her personal confrontation with the ancient texts. I shall therefore not attempt exhaustive accounts of the contents of the plays, still less exhaustive interpretations of their meaning. Rather, I shall ask the reader to accompany the last two chapters by a reading of each play as we arrive at it. For orientation's sake I shall include an outline of the play concerned, but this will not be so much a plot summary as a scenario, a working model of the tragedy in performance; the emphasis will be laid on the climactic moments, at which all our poet's resources tend to converge: verse, imagery, stage action, music, dance. I shall also try to account for certain other aspects of the plays that will not be immediately apparent from the texts themselves, notably the mythological and historical backgrounds. At the end of the process, however, these works are and should be the reader's possession, in exactly the same degree as they are mine.

VI THE ANCIENT UNIVERSE

The Persians

THE PERSIANS IS NOT MERELY THE EARLIEST SURVIVING PLAY by Aeschylus: it is also the simplest to follow, once certain basic principles of his dramaturgy are understood. The most important of those principles, from which he never departed at any stage of his extant work, may best be introduced by means of a diagram. An Aeschylean dramatic work tends to progress:

> from verbal to visual;
> from ambiguity to clarity;
> from human to divine.

That is, Aeschylus regularly moves from an initial situation on the human level, expounded primarily through words, and therefore with all the ambiguity inherent in words, toward a climax in which the divine forces that have been operating behind the human events are made clear, in some form, to the unerring sense of sight. Even in *Prometheus Bound* and its associated fragmentary plays that pattern seems only to have been varied to the extent that the initial situation was already set on the divine (or Titanic) level; what little we know of the sequel suggests that in this case a fearsome ambiguity in the divine order itself may finally have been resolved by the visual token of the Garland.

The specialized account of the early scenes of *The Persians*
that was given in chapter 3 was simply designed to show the
nature of Aeschylus' theatrical medium, without much reference to the content or development of the plot. In that opening movement, in fact, they are conveyed almost entirely
through verbal exposition. The following outline of the play
will indicate how, gradually, the meaning of the themes and
events evoked in words is given absolute and terrible definition by visual apparitions. A Chorus of Persian lords enters
with a triumphant chant that merges into a triumphant song
and dance; as far as line 107 its major theme is the wealth
and majesty of the great force that King Xerxes has led against
Greece. Already, however, shadows pass here and there
across the song: the days stretch on, and still no news has
come from the host (lines 8–11, 61–63). At line 108, still in
mid-song, total darkness succeeds the shadows, as the
Chorus suddenly remembers the deceitfulness of God, and
how Infatuation (*ātē*) can blandly tempt mankind into her
inescapable net. From that moment until the end of the song
(line 139) all is wailing, for the Chorus now envisages the
possibility of the loss of the host, the Persian cities emptied
of their menfolk, the mourning of the delicate Persian ladies.
The entrance of the Queen Mother (line 150) brings more
doubts, and increasingly specific ones. She has been troubled
by thoughts of the vulnerability of great wealth and of the
danger to Xerxes. This night she has had a dream that por-
tends his defeat and disgrace; then, rising from her bed to
avert the omen by sacrifice, she has seen in broad daylight an
unnatural thing, a little falcon swooping and slashing at a
mighty eagle. Gradually the atmosphere of the play has thus
been loaded with dread; we have fully entered into the world
of Aeschylean humanity.

The storm of disaster is unpent at line 246, where a Per-

sian messenger enters. The Messenger, like many an Aeschylean actor, is both more and less than an ordinary human
being: less, because he is given no individual traits whatever;
more, because out of mere words he can create an overpowering vision of vast landscapes and events. In his great
series of speeches, lasting, with relatively brief interruptions
by the Chorus and Queen, until line 514, the battle of Salamis
is fought and disastrously lost by the fleet of the Persians;
some of their greatest lords are trapped and massacred on an
islet in Salamis strait; and their starving and demoralized
army, under Xerxes, plods back through the hostile landscapes of northern Greece and Thrace suffering fearful losses.
By the time of the Messenger's exit the tragic action of *The
Persians*, on the human level, is in effect complete. It will be
noticed that not one of the speakers or singers who have actually appeared in the theater so far has had the least influence on the progress of that action. They can only dread,
mourn, and bear witness. The causes of the event, like the
event itself, lie far away in space and time. To discover, define, and realize them will be the business of the rest of the
play, and this process will be effected to an increasing extent
by visual means.

Nobles and Queen turn to the dead in their quest for
understanding. The ghost-raising scene (lines 598–680), in
which Xerxes' father, Darius, is conjured out of his tomb-
mound by the methodical offerings of the Queen and the
frantic dance and song of the Chorus, is one of the most
spectacular as well as the most eerie scenes in Aeschylus.
Finally, the dead sovereign stands at the top of the mound,
wearing the full regalia of a Persian emperor. This visual revelation is the medium for the great spiritual revelation of the
play, for in his ensuing speeches (lines 681–842) Darius accounts for the disaster at Salamis in the light of the cosmos

and its laws. This he is empowered to do not merely because
of his wisdom as the greatest king in an illustrious line of
kings, but because he is now a god—a god among the dead.
In this scene the ancient universe and its workings open up
before us.

The play's coda (lines 909–1046) is dominated by yet another visual embodiment of the remote, of that which up to
now has been known to us only in words and in a name.
King Xerxes himself enters, his royal robes torn to shreds (the
sharp visual contrast with the brilliant figure of his invincible
father in the previous scene does not escape us), and there
follows a wild sung-and-danced antiphony of mourning between him and the Chorus. Very near its end, at Xerxes' bid-
ding, the Chorus members rend their own magnificent robes
(line 1060). Thus Aeschylus has contrived to reenact symbol-
ically at the heart of the Persian realm, and before our very
eyes, the shame that befell the Persians at far-off Salamis.

Such is the bare outline of the verbal-visual action of *The
Persians*. Before we proceed to consider the play as an illustration of Aeschylus' dramaturgy in general, and as an exposition of the archaic universe, it will be well to address a
problem which has (I think) unduly distracted some of its
critics from those aspects. *The Persians'* subject matter, as is
well known, is unique in extant Attic tragedy in that it centers
on what we should call a historical event. Aeschylus' choice
of it, however, was perhaps not so great a departure from the
sphere of myth as it has sometimes been made to appear. The
fact was that the great Persian invasion of 480–79 B.C. made
a unique impact on the Greek imagination. Fifth-century
Greek lyric poets, wall painters, and sculptors, who, like the
tragedians, traditionally worked through mythology alone to
express their visions of life, similarly made an exception for
the Persian Wars, for these were felt at once to possess the

same exemplary and universal quality as the myths inherited from the far past. *The Persians* is not a "historical drama" in the sense that, say, a Shakespearean history play is; the only passage in it that really squares with the historical facts as they are known from other sources is the account of the actual engagement at Salamis, the rest being to a great extent free invention. (For instance, Xerxes seems not to have returned to his capital until after the entire campaign was over; he remained in Asia Minor for a full year after the naval battle.) In all significant respects it is a tragedy, neither more nor less, and as such will serve as well as any of Aeschylus' extant works to introduce his basic methods.

One fundamental principle of his work, the tendency to move from primarily verbal poetry toward a culmination that is largely expressed in what we may call visual poetry, has already been demonstrated in our account of this play. Allied to this is a remarkable poetic technique that may be called, for short, patterned imagery: the construction of sequences of images, or even just of repeated key words, that may extend across an entire play (or across an entire trilogy, if the *Oresteia* is anything to go by), evolving in their significance and in some instances even reversing their significance in sympathy with the movement of the action. Nothing precisely like this technique is found in any other ancient Greek poetry, earlier or later than Aeschylus; perhaps the closest analogy to it is to be found more than twenty-two centuries later in the leitmotiv technique of Richard Wagner, who was in fact a devotee of our poet. Again, *The Persians* exhibits in relatively simple form a standing tendency in Aeschylus' work. Here the most striking example of patterned imagery is *the rending of clothing*. That idea is first floated in the Chorus's fantasy of a defeated Persia at line 125, where it fears lest "rending assault the rich linen robes" of the Persian ladies. At line 199 the Queen tells how Xerxes "rips the robes about his body," if only in her dream; at line 468, however, Xerxes in very truth (according to the Messenger) "ripped his robes and wailed aloud" as he saw the massacre of his nobles on the islet. In the passage 832–51, the idea assumes its full symbolic importance in the tragedy. The ghost of Darius, with its supernatural vision, knows that "about his [Xerxes'] body the rents of richly colored robes show their broken threads," and tells the Queen to fetch the proper regalia for him on his return; and the Queen, leaving on this mission, laments above all "the dishonor of the clothing about my son's body." One realizes that in the Persian culture (as in others—one recalls *King Lear*, or the term for the Scottish Crown Jewels, "the Honours of Scotland") the regalia are identified with the dignity of the office and the realm. A king in torn robes is a torn, dishonored king. In the finale, as we have seen, Xerxes is presented to our eyes with his clothing indeed in rags; before our eyes also, in the closing stanzas of the great lament that follows his entrance, the counselors of the Persian Empire tear their own robes apart. The dishonor is complete and universal.

In this instance the patterned imagery closely follows, and emphasizes, the contours of the entire action: from vague premonitions at the beginning, to a specific dream, to reported fact, to onstage manifestion. There are other sequences of repeated images or words that do not issue finally in visual reality as that sequence does. They are less easy to point out to a reader who has to depend on translations, because few translators, for good stylistic reasons, have attempted to carry them over systematically into English. One example at least, however, deserves to be given in full, not merely for its own sake but also as a reminder of Aeschylus' extraordinarily fine control over his verbal medium—he is one of the few poets in the Western tradition whose command of that medium might remind one of a great composer's exact command of music. Let us follow the fortunes of two, in themselves, unremarkable words, "full" and "empty" (with their cognates) in *The Persians*. In the opening chant the hosts advancing on Greece are "innumerable in their fullness" (line 40). Then, in the Chorus's fantasy of disaster, the capital city of Sousa is envisaged as "man-emptied" (line 119), while in the same sentence a "woman-filled crowd" shrieks and tears its robes (lines 123–24). From that point of temporary union the two word-sequences diverge: "full" recurs at lines 235, 272 ("full with the bodies of ill-destined dead are the shores of Salamis!"); 334, 342, 352 (Xerxes "gloried in the fullness of his fleet"); 413, 420, 421, 429–30 (the Messenger could not in ten days "fill out the fullness of our sorrows"), 432, and 477; "empty" recurs at 549 ("all Asia emptied!"), 718, 730 (the "man-emptiness" of Sousa), and 761. Only near the end do the two converge again: Xerxes, says the ghost of Darius (lines 803–04), "By empty hopes persuaded, leaves behind / A fullness of choice warriors." Although that is the final appearance of either word, it is possible that the *thought* reaches its culmination in the sinister lines 923–24, where the Chorus scornfully calls Xerxes "he who has stuffed Hell with corpses."

Thus pulled out of their contexts and coolly enumerated, these and similar word-sequences may perhaps appear artificial or even clumsy, but that is not the effect they seem to have in practice on a reader or hearer of *The Persians*. Indeed, it takes a well-practiced listener to notice them consciously at all. One might read *The Persians* many times over before one could identify the subliminal source of the feeling of hollowness—hollowness of human pride, hollowness of empire— with which one is left at the play's end. But further discussion of the technique of patterned imagery will best await the section on the *Oresteia*, where it is to be observed at its most sophisticated stage. The time has come to consider *The Persians* in its relation to our leading topic: the cosmos and its workings, as they are implied in Aeschylus' successive plays.

Why did the catastrophe come about? One way and another the entire universe was involved in the defeat at Salamis, from the heart of Xerxes outward to infinity, but our quest may best begin from the solemn formulation uttered by Darius' ghost in lines 818–22. The wisdom of Darius rests on the authority of both the great divine realms. He is now a subject of Earth and a prince among the gods below (liness 629, 640–41, 688–92); but at the same time he is perfectly well informed about the counsels of the supernal gods, notably of Zeus (lines 739–41, 800–02); there is no hint in this episode, or anywhere in *The Persians,* of any incompatibility between the two groups. In 818–22 he is reflecting on the effects of the defeat at Salamis: it will be followed by the failure of the entire expedition, culminating (in 479 B.C.) in the bloody rout of the Persian army at Plataea. On that field, he says:

> The mounds of voiceless corpses shall yet warn
> The eyes of men, to the third-born generation,
> That mortals may not think above their state;
> For *hybris*, ripening, bears its crop, the wheat-ear
> Of *ātē*; and reaps a harvest all of tears.

The doctrine that Darius formulates here is actually as old as the oldest surviving Greek poetry. It is implicit, for instance, in the action of the sixteenth book of the *Iliad*, where Patroclus neglects it to his ruin. It is made explicit by several Greek poets who composed a century and more before Aeschylus, including the Athenian Solon, who refers to it in terms

very like those used by Darius here and in other passages of
our play. The sum of the doctrine is this: enduring happiness
and prosperity—the Greek word covering both is *olbos*—belong to the gods alone. For a mortal, *olbos* is a temporary and
fragile acquisition, and perilous too, for it is apt to induce the
condition of *hybris* ("insolence" or "pride"); this in turn, unless checked, will issue in *ātē*. This last term is generally translated as "infatuation," but there is no single English word
that corresponds to its full range of meanings. It signifies,
according to context, both the psychological state of "infatuation," the loss of judgment that leads one to forget the limits
imposed by the condition of being human; and the objective
outcome of that loss of judgment, namely "disaster."

Such is the archaic doctrine on the relative conditions of
God and Man. It seems to embody very ancient feelings on
the subject, which were not by any means confined to the
Greeks. Yet to the early-fifth-century Greeks, and not least
(as we saw above) to their artists in all mediums, it was perfectly exemplified on the grandest possible scale by the course
and outcome of Xerxes' invasion. Xerxes had coveted a greatness exceeding the limits laid down for mortality; and that
which was immortal had struck back. But who, in fact, are
the immortal guarantors of the doctrine? A line or two after
the passage just quoted Darius names one of them, at least
(lines 824–28):

> Let no man underrate his present fortune,
> Spilling great prosperity [*olbos*] in his lust for more:
> Zeus sits above us as the punisher
> Of thoughts that rise too high, a grim accountant.

In lines 532–36 and 740, Zeus is again held responsible for the
destruction of the expedition, and in line 762 Darius attributes

to him the foundation of the Persian royal power. Yet far more often in the play the source of the calamity is described as "a god" or "the gods" (*theos, theoi,* e.g., 454, 604), or, even more vaguely, as "a spirit" or "the spirits" (*daimōn, daimones,* e.g., 472, 1005). Apart from Zeus, only a few specific powers emerge from this cloud of punitive divinity. Xerxes, says Darius, has chained "the sacred Hellespont" for the passage of his army seeking to check the current of the Bosporus, "the stream of God" (lines 745–46); a mere mortal, he has tried to master Poseidon (line 750). At the crossing of the frozen river Strymon during their terrible retreat, the Persian troops salaam in vain to Sky and Earth: the Sun-God melts the ice, and many of them perish in the waters of that "holy river" (lines 495–507). The very soil of Greece is hostile to the invaders (lines 792–94). In short, the entire cosmos, visible and invisible, has united under the leadership of Zeus to enforce the ancient law.

At lines 739–41 and again at 800–04, Darius reveals another factor in the destruction of the expedition. Divine oracles had long predicted not merely the naval defeat at Salamis but also the land battle at Plataea in the following year. They were apparently *conditional* oracles, to the effect that when a Persian king should mount an amphibious invasion of Greece all these disasters would ensue. Darius is shocked to hear from the Queen that Zeus should have fulfilled those oracles so soon, and through the decision of his son, Xerxes: "for I was sure that the Gods would accomplish them only after a long time" (lines 740–41). But why should it have been Xerxes and no other who set in motion the sequence of events that had long been stored up in fate? In his next line Darius seems to supply the answer: ". . . and yet, when a man is eager in himself, God (*theos*) joins with him!" Against this, however, we have to weigh another passage in the same scene, at the point where the Queen has just told Darius about Xerxes' bridge across the Hellespont (lines 723–25):

> *Darius:* Did he really achieve that—the barring of the mighty Bosporus?
> *Queen:* It is so; perhaps one of the Spirits (*daimones*) joined with his will.
> *Darius:* Ah me! It was a mighty Spirit indeed that came upon him, so that his thoughts should not be right!

We face an enigma here—an enigma of our mortal existence that in fact remains unsolved—but this at least is clear: there is an interaction, whichever way you define it, between the powers of the universe and Xerxes' will.

Although the cosmos implied in *The Persians* is described in terms that belong to an alien millennium, its essential characteristics and the dilemmas that it poses may not seem, on reflection, to be so far remote from universal human experience. There continues to exist some highly important relationship between one's actions and sufferings, on the one hand, and, on the other, the great forces of the natural environment, the momentum built up in the past history of one's family and society, and one's will as an individual. To determine that relationship would be to see all. That is not likely to happen in this existence; otherwise our own lives, not to mention the social policies and penal laws of our communities, would not be in their present confusion. But to be aware of the complexity and immensity of the forces that together act on and in any human being—that is at least a step forward out of helpless ignorance. *The Persians* seems designed to bring before its audience, and all audiences, a reminder of that complexity and immensity. It is something far more than a monument to that struggle in the straits of Salamis long ago.

The Seven Against Thebes

Aeschylus is the terror of systematizers. *Tragoidia* was not yet in his time a clearly defined art form; not yet did it bear the tremendous load of connotations that it has acquired for us during the passage of twenty-four centuries. We have, of course, no record of the way in which our poet went to work on the composition of a drama. One may imagine, however, that his mind would range freely across the vast world of myth that he shared with his fellow citizens, seeking the story that might in some way reflect the realities of human life and society, as he then perceived them. Once he had found the right legend, he would think up the dramatic shape to fit that legend. There were as yet no rules of thumb—no five-act law, for instance, no solemn prescriptions for the dramatic unities. The drama was to be custom-tailored to the myth. In this process of ever fresh experiment Aeschylus might indeed (as he did in *The Libation-Bearers*) come up with a plot and play-shape that resemble, at least on the surface, the form of tragedy as later practiced by Sophocles and desiderated by Aristotle. Most of his play-shapes, however, were and remain simply unique, not merely in Greek tragedy as a whole but even in Aeschylean tragedy. Nothing that one had seen or heard in *The Persians*, for instance, could have prepared one for anything in the least resembling the central scene of *The Seven Against Thebes*, a scene conditioned by the fact that in the ancient Theban legend here concerned, and in that legend alone, seven champions attacked a seven-gated city. Similarly, each legend that Aeschylus dramatized seems to have evoked from him its own uniquely appropriate kind of song, its own imagery patterns, and even in some degree its own style. Almost the only restricting factors seem to have been the verbal-visual medium of the contemporary Attic theater and the poet's undeflectable pursuit, through the myth, of the realities of the human condition. "I possessed nothing," says the Poet in the *Prologue in the Theater* to Goethe's *Faust*, "and yet that nothing was enough: the urge toward truth, and the delight in fable." That paradox illuminates much in ancient Greek culture, but not least, I think, the *tragoidia* of Aeschylus.

The production record shows that *The Seven Against Thebes* was the last unit in a tragic trilogy that covered the fate of a great royal house over three generations. It was preceded by *Laius* and *Oedipus* and was followed, characteristically, by a satyr-play entitled *Sphinx*, which must have relaxed the audience's tensions by guying one of Oedipus' still most famous heroic achievements. The fragments that actually survive from *Laius* and *Oedipus* are very scanty, but a good deal about their contents can be inferred from backward references in *The Seven Against Thebes* (these mostly occur in its latter part, from line 653 onward, and especially in the song that follows Eteocles' final exit, lines 720–91). The following story outline of the lost part of the trilogy results with a fair certainty. King Laius of Thebes, visiting Apollo's sanctuary at Delphi, was three times warned by the god that he might keep his city safe if he died without begetting children (lines 742–49). This oracle he disobeyed, through what is described in one passage of *The Seven Against Thebes* as "his own unwisdom" (line 750), and in another as "ill-wisdom" (802). He lay with his wife (not named in the surviving texts; probably Aeschylus, like the other Attic tragedians, would have known her as Jocasta), and she gave birth to a son, Oedipus. The infant was exposed to die in the wilds, enclosed in an earthenware jar (that detail is preserved by a fragment of *Laius*, M 171), but somehow survived to adulthood. At a place called the Split Way (S 88) he encountered his father, Laius, and killed him. Coming afterward to Thebes, unrecognized, he won great glory by

ridding it of the man-eating monster, the Sphinx. He then
married Laius' widowed queen, not understanding that he
was thus to "sow the holy plowland of his own mother, where
he was born" (*Seven Against Thebes*, lines 753–54). The only
remaining hint of the reasons for their marriage, in the Aeschylean version, is: "Madness joined the bridal pair; their
minds were full of destruction" (lines 756–57). When Oedipus
at last "came to a sane understanding of that unhappy wedding" (lines 778–79), he blinded himself, and also laid a furious curse on his sons. We do not know the fate of his queen
in the Aeschylean version; only that she was "the unhappiest
of women that ever bore children" (lines 926–28).

Several passages in the extant third play (lines 727–33,
788–90, 816–19, 906–09, 940–43) combine to indicate that
Oedipus' curse on his sons, presumably uttered toward the
end of *Oedipus*, took the form of a riddle. Its exact wording is
not recoverable, but the drift must have been like this: *This
curse I lay on you: both of you shall inherit, in equal shares, the
wealth and the territory of Thebes; and the allotter of the shares shall
be a stranger from the sea!*

Thus, by the time *The Seven Against Thebes* opens, a mysterious and terrible potential of evil has accumulated, threatening both the city and its royal house. Apollo's oracle, long
ago, hinted that if Laius should beget children the city itself
might not survive. The royal family's history for three generations has been one of great glory and—an ominous fact in
itself for anyone who has seen *The Persians*—of overabundant
prosperity, *olbos* (lines 769–71). Each of the two earlier generations has committed acts of folly or passion, the ultimate
consequences of which are not yet known. Above all, that
riddling curse of Oedipus, still unexplicated, hangs over the
family as the play begins.

For two-thirds of its length this culminating play of the

tragic trilogy is comparable to a concerto: the clear solo instrument, the voice of Eteocles, plays against the massed orchestra of the city, represented by the Chorus of young
Theban women. Until the catastrophic change at line 653,
there is a counterpoint between the two different melodies,
Eteocles being calm and reasonable in the face of peril, while
the Chorus is in panic and despair; after that moment they
virtually exchange melodies, with amazing musical effect; on
Eteocles' exit at line 719, the solo part falls silent, forever.

In the opening section of the play (to line 180), the very
existence of Thebes is seen to be in deadly danger. Eteocles'
brother Polynices, whom he has driven into exile (line 638),
has amassed a great army in the city of Argos and has arrived
with it before the walls of Thebes, to take back the throne by
force. Of course, we never see that army or its seven mighty
champions, but such is the magic of Aeschylus' poetry—
above all in the choral songs and in the speeches of the Messenger—that we soon feel their threatening presence as powerfully as if they were onstage. The first words in the play are
spoken by a confident and decisive Eteocles, who calls on a
crowd of assembled Thebans to defend their city. Like a
helmsman high on a ship's poop, "swaying the rudder-oar,
not resting his eyelids in sleep," he alone bears the responsibility to give the proper orders in this crisis. This image of
the besieged community as a ship in a squall will reecho
through most of the play, having a special appropriateness to
a Greek city-state tight within its walls, around which "the
land-billow of an army roars" (line 64). But Aeschylus would
not be Aeschylus if he envisaged human beings alone as
rocked in that storm. "Give aid," says Eteocles to the crowd,
"both to your city and to the altars of the gods of this place,
that their honors may never be erased, and to your children,
and to Earth your mother and most dear nurse; for it is she

who nursed you when you crept as infants on her loving plain, completely accepting all the troubles of child-care" (lines 14–19). A little later, when the Thebans have dispersed to man the battlements and a Messenger has brought news that the enemy attack is imminent, Eteocles utters a solemn prayer in which the same human and divine entities are included, but with one most sinister addition (lines 69–72):

> O Zeus, and Earth, and Gods who hold our city,
> And Curse, potent Erinys of my father!
> Do not uproot the city from its base,
> I pray! Let it not perish utterly,
> Sacked by its enemies!

The second of those lines comprises the only mention of Oedipus' riddling curse that occurs in the first half of the play, but its dread presence is firmly established here at the outset. The Olympian gods, on the other hand, are visibly represented from beginning to end of *The Seven Against Thebes*. In assessing its total theatrical impact, one must bear in mind that the stage set, to be thought of as the Theban acropolis (line 240), included a silent assembly of divine images. (Several passages in the choral song, lines 78–180, as well as Eteocles' words at 258, indicate that they could be seen and indeed touched there onstage, rather than just being left to the audience's imagination).

At line 78 the chorus of women floods into the *orchēstra* in utter panic—a panic emphasized not only by the frantic words of their song but also, to judge by the meter, in their music and dancing. The song is composed almost throughout in the agitated meter called the dochmiac, which was reserved by Aeschylus and the other Attic tragedians for passages of the most violent emotion. Its first thirty lines, in particular, indicate a wild disorder in the dancing; for, unlike almost all

other Aeschylean choral song, they are not even divided up
into precisely responding stanzas, strophes, and antistrophes
(literally, "turns" and "counterturns"; this ancient terminol-
ogy must be choreographic in origin rather than poetic or
musical). To these women and their passionate supplications
to the images is contrasted (from line 181) the stately figure
of Eteocles, still in his capacity of conscientious and decisive
leader. He calms the frenzy of the women, telling them that
their screams can only demoralize the Theban soldiers. Let
them leave those images alone, and content themselves with
vowing offerings to the gods in the event of victory! For the
only immediate business is victory, and that depends entirely
on brave menfolk and strong walls. Thus briefly summarized,
Eteocles' words to the women might seem to express exactly
what his duty as king requires in these desperate circumstances. The common sense and self-reliance that he here
displays and urges on others are, one may recall, the same
qualities that enabled Oedipus, in Sophocles' version of the
story, to baffle and defeat the Sphinx. Is it possible that Aeschylus' Oedipus, as shown in the lost preceding play, was
similar in this respect, and that to the original audience Eteocles would seem in these early scenes to be speaking with the
voice of his father as he had been at the height of his glory?

   And yet the *tone* in which Eteocles delivers his advice to
the women may be very significant. There is, if not outright
lack of respect, at least a certain coolness in his attitude to
the gods and their ever-present images. Even more disturb-
ing, perhaps, is his attitude toward the women—and not
merely these women, but all women. For them he shows a
passionate contempt. They are "unbearable creatures" (line
181). Who could ever live with a woman, in evil times or
good? "When she is winning, there's no converse with her
boldness; when she panics, she's an even greater evil to her

house and city" (lines 187–90). Now, on the whole, noto-
riously, Greek society and literature were male-oriented to an
extent scarcely paralleled by any Western culture since. But
it is not often noticed that in the Attic tragedians, at least, to
condemn women as a class, to reject the feminine outright,
is regularly a sure sign of a flawed character and impending
disaster. Sophocles' Creon in *Antigone*, Euripides' Pentheus in
The Bacchae, and above all Euripides' Hippolytus, all revile the
entire sex of women, and all suffer cruel fates. Aeschylus,
who of all the three great tragedians came to be most preoccupied with the feminine as a major power in the universe
(as will be seen in the next chapter), cannot have attributed
similar, and indeed even more violent, feelings to Eteocles
just casually. In this scene with the women, the first hairline
crack seems to open up in Eteocles' character and destiny.

By the end of the scene, however, Eteocles regains his
balance. He announces briefly that he will assign seven champions, including himself, to defend the seven gates of Thebes,
and leaves the scene for this purpose (lines 283–87). After a
choral ode (lines 288–368) in which the Chorus, now left to
itself, envisages the destruction of the city in all its terrible
details, Eteocles returns just in time to meet the Messenger,
who by now has spied out the exact dispositions of the at-
tackers. We have reached the massive central episode, generally called the Shield Scene, of *The Seven Against Thebes* (lines
369–719).

Perhaps never in the history of the theater have such
complex and powerful dramatic effects been brought about by
such economical means as in the Shield Scene. There are three
participants, who never physically interact, so far as one can
tell from the text: the Messenger, progressively word-painting
the terrifying scene unfolding outside the city walls, the circle
of violence tightening around Thebes; Eteocles, confronting

the Messenger and cooly retorting to each word-picture with apt word-pictures of his own, in which he ridicules the threats of the enemy and emphasizes the steadiness of the Theban champions; and, to complete the triangular grouping, the Chorus, intermittently singing and dancing out the fears within the city. The besiegers, the besieged city and its people, the defending soldiery, and the seven captains on all sides, are all conjured up to the imagination—by three voices. One has to bear in mind that the scene begins in mutual ignorance. Eteocles, of course, knows which Theban champion he has assigned to each of the seven gates, but has yet to learn even the identities of the seven enemy champions, let alone their exact stations. The Messenger, on the other hand, knows which gate has fallen to each enemy champion through their drawing of lots, but is quite unaware that Eteocles has made any corresponding dispositions at all (see, for instance, lines 395 and 435). He simply enumerates each of those champions one by one, along with the gate to which he has been assigned, in a series of seven speeches. To each of these speeches, in turn, Eteocles replies by naming the Theban champion whom he has stationed at the gate concerned.

For five of the resultant seven pairs of speeches all goes well, as far as Eteocles and Thebes are concerned. Gate after gate, bolthole after bolthole, is blocked off by an enemy champion, as magnificently and terrifyingly described by the Messenger. Here the furious Tydeus advances; we seem to be looking full into his great shield, bearing its symbol of night and death, the full moon, "most reverend of the stars, Night's glaring eye" (line 390). Next the Messenger describes Capaneus, the great blasphemer against the Olympian gods, who carries a shield with another threatening device: a torch-bearing man, with the inscription, "I'll burn the city!" Then, still pictured through the Messenger's words, advance other ogre-like figures, each headed for his allotted gate. Eteoclus (*sic*; his only connection with Eteocles lies in the sound of his name) carries on his shield an armored warrior mounting a scaling-ladder. Hippomedon brandishes "a mighty threshing-floor" of a shield (line 489), on which the monstrous Typhon, the archetypal rebel against Zeus, snorts smoke shot with flame. As sinister as any of them is the fifth champion, Parthenopaeus, "Girl-Face," whose lovely, boyish appearance belies his bestial heart; his shield insultingly recalls the moment of Thebes's greatest terror and shame, for its device is a Theban in the grip of the Sphinx. Yet all these challengers and the symbols on their shields, described in words, are successfully matched, likewise in words, by Eteocles' responding speeches. Against Tydeus, for instance, he applies the very ancient device of "retorting" the iconography of his shield against its bearer: that imaged night will prove to fall on the eyelids of Tydeus himself (lines 400–07)! Or again, he points out how the enemies' lot-drawing and his own dispositions have between them matched Eteoclus' Typhon against a shield showing Typhon's victorious enemy, Zeus, which is borne by the Theban champion Hyperbius (lines 508–20).

At the same time the tension builds. After five gates have been accounted for, the hearers still do not know at which of the seven Eteocles himself will fight (that he is to be one of the Theban champions we know from line 283), or against whom. The full list of the seven enemy champions has nowhere been revealed; yet as the options, like the gates, are blocked off one by one, fear mounts that Eteocles' brother Polynices may be included in it, and that Eteocles—through his own carefully laid military plans and the fortunes of the enemies' lot-drawing—may yet find himself locked into a frat-

ricidal duel. More and more, the memory of Oedipus' riddling
curse may tease the spectator, much as the riddle of the coming of Birnam Wood to Dunsinane teases a spectator of *Mac-
beth*.

In the sixth pair of speeches the atmosphere of the play
changes abruptly: Thebes is faced with a challenge more formidable than any that has been described up until now; Eteocles is brought to the highest point of his nobility, in sharp
contrast to all that is to follow. The Messenger announces that
the sixth enemy champion is the valiant and blameless seer
Amphiaraus, who (as the ancient legend told) was tricked into
promising that he would join this expedition against Thebes.
His honor would not let him break that promise, even though
he well knew that he was fated to die before the Theban walls.
The shield that Amphiaraus carries into battle, just like all the
other shields described by the Messenger, is an emblem of
the man—*is* the man. This is the Messenger's account of it
(lines 591–94):

> The circle of his shield bore no device:
> He wishes not to seem best, but to *be* so,
> Reaping a furrow deep-plowed through his mind,
> From which the crop of noble thinking springs.

That second line has perhaps never been surpassed as an
epigrammatic description of a truly virtuous man. It has lived
a rich life of its own in the intellectual history of the Western
world—especially since Plato, of all people (for Plato in his
philosophic capacity was no lover of Attic tragedy), adopted
it as the basis of his search for the just man and the just
society, in his *Republic*. Attic tragedy should never be confused
with philosophy; its approach to the realities is profoundly different, and indeed we often have to think away many subsequent philosophy-dominated centuries before we can read

its message. Yet in many senses it was the deep-plowed fur-
row from which philosophy would later spring.

Eteocles' reply to the Messenger's account of Amphiaraus
shows him at his finest; at this point one may even feel that
he matches the nobility of the warrior-seer. He expresses no
hatred against this enemy, and no contempt, simply deep pity
for a virtuous man, "a hero temperate, just, brave, and pious,
a mighty prophet" (lines 610–11), who has been trapped into
his doom. Even so, Eteocles does not forget his kingly duty
to reassure the Messenger and the Chorus. This most dan-
gerous of opponents, he says, is probably destined to fall even
before he reaches his allotted gate, but if he gets so far he will
be met there by a superb spearman, the Theban Lasthenes.
Only one shadow falls across the episode of Amphiaraus,
although for the time being Eteocles seems to be unconscious
of it: his brother Polynices is here mentioned for the first time
in *The Seven Against Thebes*. In lines 576–86 the Messenger
describes how Amphiaraus has loudly abused Polynices, asking how the gods can ever approve of one who "hurls in an
alien army to sack the city of his fathers and the Gods of his
race. What kind of Justice (*dikē*) is it that shall quell the
mother-fountain?" The lines, at this stage, are tantalizing.
They convey the great seer's understanding that the attack on
the city, its gods, and its natural features (for this trio, compare Eteocles' speeches in the Prologue) is contrary to justice
and must fail. They bring Polynices' name and presence very
pointedly to our attention. Yet they still do not reveal whether
or not he has drawn one of the seven lots that would set him
among the enemy champions.

Now comes the Messenger's last speech. Before the seventh gate, he says, is your own brother Polynices, praying
that he may meet you in battle and either die beside you or
drive you into exile. On his shield is shown a woman in-

scribed *Dikē*, who is leading an armed warrior. "Such are the devices that the enemy has contrived," concludes the Messenger; "now *you yourself judge* whom you think fit to send. There is no way in which you can fault *me* for my work as herald; it is for *you yourself to judge* how to steer the city" (lines 649–52). The words here italicized leave no room for doubt about the innocent Messenger's understanding of the situation. He is under the impression, as he seems to have been throughout the Shield Scene, that Eteocles' choice of each successive Theban champion is unrestricted by any prior decisions, and that here too, in this last and worst of the choices, he is free to use his own judgment.

But the very first words that issue from the mouth of Eteocles as the Messenger leaves the scene (lines 653ff.) show that there is now no longer anything left in him that is capable of judging at all. Where there was once a responsible individual, the curse of Oedipus, the madness of the entire line, and the vengeance of Apollo have now taken over. Somehow those forces have combined, as he now recognizes, to maneuver him and his brother into facing each other at the seventh gate. The lot-drawing on the enemy side—here one must bear in mind the Greek belief that lot-drawing was no matter of chance, but an appeal to the divine will—has brought Polynices there; in ignorance of that, and in the fulfillment of his duty as king and commander, Eteocles has long ago assigned himself to the same station. He concludes that the curse of Oedipus has "boiled over" in him (line 709), and he simply capitulates to it. The Chorus, now assuming the reasonable role that was formerly his, can do nothing to deflect him: "My beloved father's black and hateful curse settles against my sere eyes that cannot weep!" (lines 695–96).

It has been suggested, I believe rightly, that throughout his final dialogue with the women Eteocles is slowly and inex-

orably arming himself for combat, in the guise of a *hoplītēs*, a
heavy-armed infantryman. The textual support for this is
found at lines 675–76, where he calls for his greaves, normally
the first item to be strapped on by a Greek warrior; and line
717, just before his exit, where he rejects the Chorus's plea
that he should not fight with the proud words, "It is not for
a man who is a *hoplītēs* to agree with that!" If the suggestion
is correct, that arming—that gradual masking of the human
form behind metal—is the only significant visual gesture in
the Shield Scene. Otherwise the long-drawn-out suspense
and the final overwhelming shock of that long episode have
been created entirely by spoken or sung poetry.

The armed figure hurries from the scene. Just out of the
spectator's view is to be imagined that gate where Eteocles is
about to fight his brother and the wall encircling Thebes, before which the fate of Thebes will be decided in the general
battle. While the women of the Chorus await the outcome,
they do all that can be done: they sing (lines 720–91). The full
meaning of Oedipus' riddle is now clear to them. The
"stranger from the sea" has proved to be iron, for in early
Greek legend (which may in this case, as in others, preserve
authentic memories of the late Bronze Age in the Greek area)
iron is an alien substance, manufactured by the Chalybes, a
mysterious people located somewhere in Russia beyond the
Black Sea. A common Greek name for that sea is simply "The
Sea," *Pontos*, a fact of which Oedipus' riddle took full advan-
tage. And this Sea-Stranger will indeed assign equal shares
in Thebes to the two brothers, for each of them shall hold just
as much Theban soil as will suffice for his grave (lines 731–
33). Both at the beginning and the end of the same song the
Chorus also recognizes, as Eteocles had recognized as early
as line 70, that the curse will be put into effect by the Erinys.
This power (or alternatively, these powers, Erinyes) already

appeared briefly in chapter 1 as the one recognized since the days of Homer and Hesiod as the executrix of oaths and curses, especially curses uttered by parents. Up until the time of Aeschylus her function is fairly clear-cut. She is a specifically *feminine* power, closely associated with our mother, the Earth, and all that Earth stands for: continuity and the inexorable preservation of the way things are, physically and morally. On the other hand, no one knows very much about her physical shape (this is very often true of earth-deities generally, as opposed to the Olympians). She possesses the decisive powers of a god, but at the same time the eerie intangibility of a poltergeist. Where she is mentioned in extant Aeschylus, she retains these ancient traits, until we reach the last play of the *Oresteia*, *The Eumenides*. There, for the first time in history so far as we know, Aeschylus gave Erinys a clear visible shape and actually let her loose in the theater, in her plural guise. If you can once *see* a power, you can negotiate and come to terms with it; and in *The Eumenides* this is done. For the present, however, in *The Seven Against Thebes*, there is no hint of such a revolutionary approach to the Erinys, nor yet of any discord between her and the gods of Olympus. She holds the place that she had always held in the archaic cosmos.

In that song of theirs, the Chorus has progressed so far in the unraveling of Oedipus' curse. The fate of the royal house now seems clear, but the Chorus still has no hint as to the fate of Thebes: "I fear that with our kings our city too may be tamed in destruction" (lines 764–65). Complete enlightenment is not reached until the reappearance of the Messenger at line 792. He brings this news: "Fallen are the boasts of the mighty [enemy], and our city sails in calm waters; in all the many shocks of the billow she took in no seas. . . . For the most, I say, all is well—at six of our gates. But the seventh gate was taken for his own by the holy Lord, Leader of Sevens, Apollo, in his fulfillment of the ancient unwisdom of Laius." Thus the two kings lie dead, "and through their mutual slaughter Earth has drunk the blood of two who sprang from one and the same seed" (lines 820–21).

From the withdrawal of the Messenger (line 821) onward there is no more unaccompanied spoken poetry in *The Seven Against Thebes* (at least in the view, which I share, that lines 1011–84 are a post-Aeschylean addition; see the Epilogue). This tragedy, and with it this trilogy, ends as *The Persians* did, in a storm of rhythmic wailing; this is centered, as the finale of *The Persians* was, on an utterly definitive visual symbol of the outcome. This time the symbol is the two corpses that are carried into the theatral area during the wild singing and dancing at lines 848–60, and remain there thenceforward. Before our eyes lies the final annihilation of the house of Laius, with all its prosperity, ambition, and folly. To translate freely the words of the Chorus (lines 947–48):

> Now underneath each body
> Shall stretch unfathomed riches,
> An endless wealth—of earth!

The Seven Against Thebes is a very much more complex work than *The Persians* of five years before. One reason, perhaps the chief reason, for this is that Aeschylus here worked on the vast scale afforded by the connected trilogy. There was room to develop the story not merely of a single event, but of the actions and passions of an entire family over three generations; and the threads spun in the lost *Laius* and *Oedipus* had to be brought together and finally interwoven in the one surviving play of the group. Yet the cosmos implied in it still seems fundamentally similar to that of *The Persians*. The universe remains one—all its divine powers, infernal and supernal, cooperating from one end to the other of the story.

We have seen, for instance, how the long chain of events initiated by the words of Apollo, a god par excellence of the bright sky, is consummated both by him (lines 800–02) and by an earth-goddess, the Erinys. The universe likewise continues to confront mankind with mysteries whose solution is learned only late and after great suffering; and which, when they are learned, bring no comfort.

VII NO-MAN'S LAND OF DARK AND LIGHT

The Suppliants

IT MAY HAVE BECOME CLEAR BY NOW THAT IN MANY WAYS
Aeschylus' work has the quality not so much of logically or-
ganized narrative as of dream—of nightmare. It may display
the superficial incoherence or even the impossibility of
dreams, their liberation from the order of time or space, their
rapid succession of frightful visions, one melting into the
other. Yet, by virtue of that very freedom from the limitations
that are imposed on the ordinary waking mind, these dramas
also possess the compulsive force of dreams. Reaching out
effortlessly through the entire sphere of our experience, they
bring back and concentrate the essence of our anxieties—or
of our hopes.

The Suppliants is perhaps the most dreamlike of all the
seven plays. In one passage, indeed, its Chorus sings in the
veritable imagery of nightmare: as the Egyptian enemy threatens to drag them off to the ships, the girls scream (lines 886–
88):

> He leads me seaward
> Like a spider step by step.
> A dream!
> A black dream!

But in truth, as we shall see, the entire exotic myth which

Aeschylus chose as the basis for this play in itself reads like a very ancient dream. Even if the tetralogy to which it belonged had survived entire, one may suspect that a massive effort of any modern person's imagination would be required to understand it. As things are, we have only the first play of the tetralogy, and our information about the development of the story in the subsequent plays is very fragmentary indeed. Even this first play is in an exceptionally poor state of preservation: the text of *The Suppliants* depends on a single Byzantine manuscript, which happens to be unusually corrupt at several crucial passages. For example, in the climactic scene at lines 825–902, much of the lyric has been reduced almost to gibberish, and the manuscript does not even make clear the identity of the Chorus's antagonist there.

Both for internal and external reasons, therefore, neither of them the fault of Aeschylus, *The Suppliants* is more difficult to interpret than any other of the seven plays. But I, for one, have never found it in the least difficult to enjoy, from the moment I first happened to read it. I delighted not only in the sheer strangeness of the landscape in which I found myself and of the figures moving in that landscape, but also in the singing. *The Suppliants* stands out from among all the other works of Aeschylus, and all other ancient tragedies, as truly a lyrical drama, excelling both in the relative length of its songs and in their intensity.

The broad outlines of the ancient saga on which the tetralogy was based can be recovered partly from Aeschylus himself (as we shall see, he alluded to it extensively in another extant play, *Prometheus Bound*) and partly from other Greek and Roman authors dating from Hesiod down to the late-antique compilers of mythological handbooks. These sources, diverse as they are, are in agreement about the major events in the story for most of its course. In the far remote mythological past, at a time when Zeus was relatively new to the government of heaven, he made love to a girl in the city of Argos, Io. When his consort, Hera, discovered this, she transformed Io into a cow, whereupon Zeus assumed the form of a bull and continued his visits. Hera retaliated by setting a monstrous watchman over Io to frustrate his attentions; this was Argus, who could keep watch in all directions, even heavenward, because his entire body was covered with eyes. Hermes slew Argus, but Hera then sent a gadfly to sting Io into motion, and the girl-cow bounded away in agony through much of Greece and Asia, until at last she reached Egypt. There, in Egypt, the tone of the saga transforms itself. We learn that, with a miraculous act of stroking (the Greek is *ephapsis*), Zeus gently begot on Io a divine child, Epaphus, whereby she became the ancestress of a resplendent line of divine beings and hero-kings. From Epaphus sprang Libye; from her, the brothers Agenor and Belus; and from Belus, in turn, the brothers Aegyptus and Danaus, who fathered fifty sons and fifty daughters (these latter known as the "Danaids"), respectively. When Aegyptus' sons pressed marriage on their cousins, Danaus embarked in a ship with the girls and sought sanctuary in Argos, the ancient home of their ancestress, Io.

Such is the state of affairs at the opening of the action of *The Suppliants*. What happens in the story after the close of that action is concisely told in Prometheus' prophecy to Io in the *Prometheus Bound*, lines 856–69, which is quoted here. Most of the later Greek and Roman versions essentially agree with this one:

[The sons of Aegyptus,] their minds aflutter with passion, like falcons closely following after doves, shall come [to Argos] hunting a marriage that should not be hunted.

Yet God shall begrudge them the girls' bodies, for Pelasgus' land shall give them welcome—a welcome of war
waged by murderous women! They shall be mastered by
a daring that watches in the night: each bride shall take
the life away from her husband, dyeing the two honed
edges of a sword in his blood (I'd wish such sex as that
upon my enemies!). Yet one alone of all the girls shall so
feel the magic of desire that she shall not kill her bedfel-
low . . . and this girl shall bear a line of kings in Argos.

All the ancient sources that name the solitary innocent Danaid
and the bridegroom whom she spared agree that they were
called Hypermnestra and Lynceus, but their agreement ceases
from that point in the story onward. We have very little evidence as to which, if any, of their diverse accounts of the
subsequent fortunes of Danaus and his daughters was
adopted by Aeschylus in his tetralogy.

The saga is one of the most outlandish and furthest removed from recognizable humanity in all Greek mythology.
Most of the figures who appear in it seem to be faded international memories of gods, or near-gods. Some interpreters
have even recognized the confused vestiges of a sky-myth in
Io (the moon?) and the many-eyed watcher Argus (the starry
heaven?). Certain ancient Greeks already equated Io with the
Egyptian goddess Isis, often represented wearing a headdress
of horns enclosing a moon, and Epaphus with the bull-god,
Apis. Libye gave her name to the vast tract of Libya; Aegyptus, his to Egypt; Danaus, his to the Greeks (who were com-
monly called Danai in the early epics). Agenor was hero-king
of the Phoenicians, while Belus' name seems to be connected
with the divine title Baal, familiar from the Bible. Nor are the
events in the saga of Io and her descendants much less surreal
than its characters, from Zeus's game of marital deception in

the Argive pasture to the abomination of the forty-nine murders at the moment of sexual union. One may well wonder
what element in it particularly attracted Aeschylus's imagination as he roamed the wilderness of legend in search of a
theme for his next offering at the Great Dionysia. There are,
in fact, fairly substantial reasons for guessing that that element may have been the pattern of *confrontation between the
male and the female* that recurs in the saga from beginning to
end. It may become increasingly evident in the course of the
present chapter that the idea of sexual confrontation assumed
a very great symbolic importance in our poet's vision of the
universe during this last phase of his career.

The imagined setting of *The Suppliants* was a place near
the Argive seacoast. Visible in the theater, to judge by lines
188–222 and some other passages, was a fairly high mound
on which were an altar and symbols representing various
Olympian gods; below it was an unconsecrated level space
(lines 508–09), presumably represented by the floor of the
orchēstra. The spectators of the play must have been thor-
oughly shaken before a word was uttered, for the Chorus of
Danaids that filed through the side entrances evidently wore
black masks (lines 154–55, 279–80) and were costumed after
the fashion of the East, in tiaras, head-veils, and richly woven
robes (122, 234–36, 431–32, with several other passages). The
only recognizably Greek items in their appearance were the
leafy boughs, garlanded with strands of wool, that each carried (lines 22–23); these were the customary tokens of sup-
plication. The number of the chorus members in this play is
uncertain. Modern estimates vary from twelve or fifteen,
which seem to have been the usual numbers in the time of
Aeschylus, to fifty, the number universally assigned to each
of the families of Danaus and Aegyptus in the ancient versions of the saga (including the references to it in Aeschylus

himself). Even if one assumes one of the lower numbers, the theatral area must have been quite crowded, since the Chorus seems to have been accompanied by a group of handmaidens equal to them in number (lines 954, 977–79, 1022). With this spectacular procession, or just behind it, entered Danaus, whose appearance was no less exotic than that of his daughters (lines 496–98).

The opening of the play, like that of *The Persians*, is entirely choral, consisting of an entry chant as far as line 39 and a danced song from 40 to 175. The Chorus's major themes here are an appeal to the protection of Zeus and to the precedent of Zeus's relations with his lover Io, long ago: may they, like her, at last find release from their tormented wanderings across the world! This latter theme will be sustained in the choral singing throughout the play, most notably in the great central ode at lines 524–99 and in the exit antiphony at 1051–73. It forms a kind of secondary plot on the lyric level, above and behind the development of the dramatic action.

That action, in itself, is relatively easy to describe in outline; our problems, as will appear later, lie rather in determining its significance. Danaus, just after the opening song ends, sees an armed force approaching and tells his daughters to ascend the mound and lay their suppliant-boughs against the symbols of the gods. Immediately after they have done so, Pelasgus, king of Argos and all Greece, enters accompanied by soldiers. In the long episode from lines 234–479, the Chorus first convinces him that despite all appearances they can claim kinship with his people through their ancestress Io; then, with much more difficulty, they prevail on him to ask his citizens to grant them asylum from their pursuers. The King leaves for the city of Argos on this mission, having sent Danaus on ahead of him to win sympathy by placing some of the suppliant-boughs on the city's altars. There follows the

majestic choral ode on Zeus and Io already mentioned (lines
524–99), after which Danaus reappears, bringing the news
that the Argive citizens in assembly have granted the
Chorus's request by an overwhelming vote. The Chorus responds with an impassioned hymn of blessing to Argos (lines
625–709). But terror strikes at this height of joy. Danaus announces that from where he stands on the top of the mound
he can see a squadron of ships standing in toward the shore.
The crews must be Egyptian, for "their black limbs stand out
clear to the eye against their white tunics" (lines 719–20); the
extraordinary vividness of this detail, as of the entire report
of a scene supposed to lie just outside the spectator's view,
may remind one of the similar techniques employed in *The
Seven Against Thebes*. Against all expectation, Aegyptus and
his sons have already caught up with the refugees. Danaus
hurries away to seek the help of the King in this crisis, and
the Chorus, again alone, bursts into a wild lament—to my
ear, one of the most moving lyrics in all of Aeschylus (lines
776–824). There follows one of those climactic epiphanies that
are so characteristic of our poet's dramaturgy. From the earliest lines of the play the audience has been *hearing* of those
cruel Egyptian pursuers; now it *sees* them, or some of them.
The state of the manuscript here, as already mentioned, is
such that students have not been able to agree on whether
the enemies who now burst into the theatral area are the sons
of Aegyptus themselves attended by a herald, or simply the
herald with a few of his henchmen; doubtfully, I here adopt
the latter view. The scene, mostly in lyric meters from lines
825 to 901, is the most violently worded in all of Aeschylus'
plays, and the actions were presumably as violent. Here is an
example of the language, to which the accompanying action
is easily imagined; at 836–42 the Herald screams (with mounting incoherence):

Hurry hurry to the ship,
Fast as your feet [can carry]!
Tugging of hair, tugging of hair,
Pricking of goads!
Murderous bloodflow,
Chop to the neck!
Hurry hurry to damnation!

The turmoil is ended only by the reappearance of the King, who sends the Herald packing, offers the Danaids secure homes in Argos, and then withdraws. At line 980 Danaus reenters with Argive soldiers to escort them to the city. In a majestic lyric finale (lines 1018–73), the Danaids leave the *orchēstra*, singing in antiphony with their handmaids; the latter plead for the cause of Aphrodite, the former reject all thought of marriage imposed against their will. In the last two stanzas of the recessional the Danaids, it seems, have the last word. They appeal for the last time to the precedent of Zeus's love for Io and his ultimate rescue of her from her torment, and pray for "victory to the Women." The dark faces, the gorgeous Eastern robes, disappear one by one through the side entrance.

All we know of the play that came next in the tetralogy is its title *Aigyptioi*, "The Egyptians." It is fair to infer from that, that the chorus here consisted of the sons of Aegyptus. The singing in this second play, then, must have been as overwhelmingly masculine in tone as that of *The Suppliants* is feminine; the antithesis between sex and sex could not have been more powerfully effected. Somewhat more is known about the third tragedy, entitled *The Danaides*. Again, the composition of its chorus can be inferred from the title: the daughters of Danaus must now have reappeared in the *orchēstra*. Thus femininity once again dominated the theater—but, there is good reason to believe, *murderous* femininity; for the eventual betrothal of the Danaids to the sons of Aegyptus (however it may have been brought about), and the orgy of bloodshed on the wedding night, were episodes so firmly established in the saga throughout antiquity from the *Prometheus* onward, that it is most unlikely that Aeschylus could have omitted them from his present dramatization of it.

Some hint of the way in which *The Danaides* opened may be preserved in a mutilated fragment of the play (S 24), where a speaker seems to be urging the singing of a dawn-song for the happy awakening of the bridegrooms. If that is a correct reading of the fragment, then the shock of the subsequent discovery of the corpses, and the emergence into the *orchēstra* of the—presumably bloodstained—Danaids, must have been overpowering. This, however, cannot be rated as more than an attractive conjecture. Much more substantial evidence about *The Danaides* is preserved in the fragment S 25, one of the most spectacular passages in Aeschylus. In this, the goddess Aphrodite has manifested herself in the theater (all we know of Aeschylus' dramaturgy would suggest that such a divine epiphany would have occurred toward the play's end). She is speaking of one of the most ancient myths of all, one that can be traced back as far as the Vedic hymns of India and forward from Aeschylus almost until the collapse of the Graeco-Roman civilization: the mating of Ouranos and Gē in the rains of spring:

> Now the pure Heaven yearns to pierce the Earth;
> Now Earth is taken with longing for her marriage.
> The rains showering from the mating Sky
> Fill her with life, and she gives birth, for man,
> To flocks of sheep and to the lifegiving wheat.
> And from that liquid exultation springs,
> Perfect, the time of trees. In this I share.

After the terrors and splendors of the tragic trilogy, invariably came the frolics of the satyr-play. In this instance, by a great stroke of good fortune, we have not merely the title, *Amymōnē*, but an ancient Greek summary of the story (S 4, introduction; M 130):

> Since the land of Argos lacked water, . . . Danaus sent his daughters to find some. In the course of her search one of them, Amymone, threw a javelin at a deer, but actually hit a sleeping satyr. Starting up from his sleep he became eager to mate with her, but then Poseidon appeared. The satyr ran away, and Amymone lay with Poseidon, who revealed to her the springs at Lerna. . . . And by Poseidon Amymone gave birth to Nauplios.

Nauplios, like so many earlier members of his mother's family from Libye onward, became an eponymous hero; his name lives on in the still thriving Argive port of Navplion. We also have a verbatim fragment of this satyr-play (S 4), a single line that may well have been spoken by Poseidon to Amymone: "Your fate is to be married; mine, to marry!"

Now in spite of the very fragmentary condition of this tetralogy, one great recurrent theme seems to emerge from all we know about it: the theme of a sexual union enforced by a male on a female who is inferior in strength or status but at last issuing happily in an illustrious offspring. It appears in the stories of Zeus and Io, that of the Danaids and their cousins (though here the happy outcome is apparently confined to the innocent Hypermnestra), and that of Poseidon and Amymone. The solemn speech of Aphrodite in *The Danaides*, against this background, seems like an exemplary variation on the same theme. Here the sexual union takes place between august equals, the primal male and the primal female in the divine genealogy of the Greeks; the first two lines of the fragment, with their symmetrical statements, emphasize that their desire is completely reciprocal, neither side compelling the other; and its issue is nothing less than the life of this planet—the life of men, animals, and plants.

The precise plot-mechanics of the entire tragic trilogy— *The Suppliants, The Aigyptioi, The Danaides*—are obviously impossible to guess at once we have passed beyond the first play. Yet its general rhythm and tendency seem fairly clear. The dominant theme from beginning to end, and even in the satyric tailpiece, *Amymōnē*, was the relationship between male and female; yet the trilogy somehow swung from a perception of that relationship as one of terror and hostility on the female side and brutal aggressiveness on the male side toward a serene vision of the creative power of mutual love between the masculine and feminine on the human, the Olympian, and, finally, the cosmic levels. Whether the murderous Danaids in Aeschylus' version, in spite of all, shared in that final peace and attained the "release from sorrow" (*Suppliants*, lines 1064–65) which they discerned and appealed to in the story of Zeus and Io, there is no knowing on the evidence we have. But there can be no question that the trilogy as a whole introduces us to a cosmos in which change can at least be envisioned as possible—change from the chaotic rule of violence and injustice to a harmony of opposite forces; and, with change, release from the ancient sorrows imposed by history and heredity. In this aspect above all, *The Suppliants* trilogy contrasts very sharply with *The Persians* and the trilogy which ends with *The Seven Against Thebes*, in which dramas we have confronted a static, inexorable cosmos, all of whose powers conspire to afflict erring humanity even to the third generation; and in the same aspect it ranks itself alongside the other works of our second group, the *Oresteia* and the *Prometheus*.

There are other features also of this tetralogy that seem

to associate it with that second group, and they are worth enumerating here. At this stage in our progress through Aeschylean drama they may appear mysterious. They should, however, increasingly make sense as we consider the two other works in the group, and above all the *Oresteia*; for, since that work is our only completely surviving tragic trilogy, it allows us to see, as the others do not, how Aeschylus might develop the meaning, or even reverse the meaning, of a given theme or character in its passage through three entire connected plays.

Most notable of these new features is the poet's fierce concentration on the actions and nature of the father and lord of the Olympian gods. In *The Persians* and *The Seven Against Thebes* Zeus is certainly a mighty power in the enforcement of the laws of the universe, but he is practically featureless. In *The Suppliants*, on the other hand, he is almost omnipresent, and in two aspects that are simply irreconcilable. In the first, he appears as the archaic, anthropomorphic, or even theriomorphic, God who casually takes his pleasure with Io at the outset of the legend. In the second, he is the transcendent being who at the culmination of that same legend brings into existence a line of gods and kings who shall found nations on three continents by means of his touch alone (a detail that may bring to mind the Creation of Adam on the ceiling of the Sistine Chapel). In *The Suppliants* both aspects are acknowledged: the first in many passages, above all lines 295–310; the second, in songs like this (lines 93–103):

> Thickforested, thickshadowed, stretch away
> The paths of his intelligence;
> Down them, impossible for the eye to see.
> He dashes men to ruin
> From the high towers of hope.

> Force is not in his armory,
> For all that a God does
> Is freed from labor. Sitting in his place
> He executes his will
> From there, from the pure throne.

Or this (524–26):

> Lord of Lords,
> Of blest most blest, of absolutes
> Most absolute power,
> Most happy Zeus!

Or this (598–99):

> For each thing, whether deed or word,
> The wisdom of his heart
> Can hasten into being.

I have selected only a few such passages (the reader may enjoy searching *The Suppliants* for more, especially in the entrance and exit songs, and elsewhere in the great central ode from which the second and third are taken), but they may be enough to indicate that this second aspect of Zeus, "whose dreams and deeds are one," has nothing in common with the first—that Zeus who has to satisfy his animals needs by assuming the form of a bull and materializing in the Argive meadows. In the play that opens *The Suppliants* tetralogy and is its solitary extant unit, the two visions of the god are presented in flat juxtaposition without comment—except for the acknowledgment that the one came later than the other. On the available evidence we cannot say, of course, whether at a later point in the trilogy the audience was permitted to understand which vision was the true one (although the analogies of the *Oresteia* and perhaps even of the Prometheus plays might suggest that this eventually came about), but even so, one fairly certain conclusion can be drawn even from what little we have: Aeschylus is now aware that two very different kinds of Zeus are possible: an ancient theriomorphic Zeus who fits perfectly into the wild landscape of primaeval legend, and a being freed from the laws of matter who might be more at home, one would say, in the realms of Platonic philosophy or of Hebrew prophecy. Not merely the cosmos (as we already saw) but also its Olympian ruler seem to be losing their old stability and certainty. We are in transition from the ancient terror of a fixed, inexorable universe to a terror of a quite different kind, and one that is ours as well as our poet's: the terror of utter and unpredictable change in Nature, God, and Man.

The Chorus of Danaids, like Zeus, is given flatly contradictory aspects in *The Suppliants,* although in this case we are in a slightly better position to conjecture the solution to the resultant riddle. "These illustrious Suppliants," observed the eighteenth-century translator R. Potter in his still very readable version of Aeschylus' extant plays, "are drawn . . . with a firmness of soul becoming their high rank, but tempered with a modest and amiable sensibility, and an interesting plaintiveness, that might have been a model even to the gentle and passionate Ovid." That is indeed elegantly said, and many a reader, whether or not of the eighteenth century, may have shared Mr. Potter's sentiments on approaching the play for the first time; I will admit that I myself first read it, during my teens, in the same light. Yet the closer one's acquaintance becomes with *The Suppliants* tetralogy and with the other works of the second group of Aeschylus' extant plays, the less one may be inclined to accept such a characterization of the Danaids. These girls are surely not, as Potter perhaps inevitably viewed them, merely dainty figures on a Wedgewood urn, dancing sweetly across a background as pure as the blue sky. They are not exactly the gentle, helpless creatures— nightingales or doves or heifers—that their own imagery and that of their father, Danaus, would persuade us that they are.

As early in *The Suppliants* as lines 21–22, an experienced listener to Aeschylus might sense some potential of evil in them. We come to Argos, they chant, bearing "these sup- pliant-daggers—these wool-wreathed boughs!" The surface meaning of the riddling phrase "suppliant-daggers" is of course innocent enough—the suppliant's token, the bough, is obviously the only weapon with which a helpless arrival can defend himself—but our poet is not exactly accustomed to pick his words at random, and the particular word for a weapon that he has picked here, *encheiridion*, has most of the connotations of "stiletto" in English. Throughout his work Aeschylus has the habit of putting into his characters' mouths loaded phrases whose true significance only becomes appar- ent, to the speakers as well as to the audience, much later in the action; one may recall the Persian lords' heavy emphasis on the wealth and power of the imperial host in the opening song of *The Persians*, to take an uncomplicated instance. The faintly sinister metaphor of *The Suppliants* 21–22 may also be an example of this practice, an almost subliminal warning of the stealthy murder that the girls are later to commit. Overtly evil, however, are their threats to commit suicide if they do not get their own way. The culmination of their lengthy plea to the wavering Pelasgus for sanctuary is the dialogue at lines 455–67, which is worth a careful reading—or, better, acting. In a series of sarcasms and riddles, the girls confront the King with a plan so blasphemous that until the last moment he simply cannot take it in: if he will not support their cause, they say, they will hang themselves from the divine symbols on the mound, thus irremediably polluting the city and land

of Argos and its very gods. Nor is that the first occasion in
the play on which they have resorted to this kind of blackmail.
At lines 154–75, toward the end of the opening song in which
they hymn the majesty of the transcendent Zeus (see lines
93–103, quoted above), they threaten the god himself: if he
will not hear them, then they will hang themselves and seek
the protection of that mirror-Zeus who rules the dead, Hades,
while infamy will fall on the Zeus of Olympus. Other sinister
features in the Danaids' character seem to be their ferocious
hatred of the sons of Aegyptus (they have a legitimate com-
plaint against their conduct, indeed, but does it justify language like that used at lines 30–36, or 511, or 529–30, for
instance?) and the charge of lack of moderation—always a danger signal in an ancient Greek context—that is leveled at them
by the Handmaids during the recessional song (line 1059).

In short, the Danaids are represented in *The Suppliants* as
gentle and murderous, moderate and excessive, pious and
blasphemous. At this stage of the trilogy one cannot make
sense of their nature any more than one can make sense of
the self-contradictory nature of Zeus. Now this seeming la-
bility, this doubleness of character, is another very important
characteristic of all the plays in the second group of Aeschylus' oeuvre. Indeed, I take an understanding of it to be indispensable to any just assessment of those plays—even of the
completely preserved *Oresteia* trilogy, let alone of the fragment
that is *Prometheus Bound*. For with this group we enter an
anxiety-ridden cosmos in which, to begin with, all phenomena are ambiguous, and every being from Zeus downward
may wear a double face. It seems that only as each trilogy
progressed out of that nightmare into the clarity of day did
the true, enduring face of things gradually revolve into the
spectator's field of vision.

One further aspect of *The Suppliants* demands mention.

In spite of its chronological location in an antiquity remote even by mythological standards, this tragedy repeatedly emphasizes the classical Athenian concept of government directly by the people. Many passages show that King Pelasgus, like any contemporary Athenian magistrate, may only act subject to the vote of the people in assembly; examples are lines 365–75 (where he first points out this constitutional fact to the uncomprehending Danaids; they are evidently under the impression that his powers are absolute, like those of an Oriental despot), 516–23, and 600–24. They are of interest to us both as students of Aeschylean drama and as remote inheritors of the democratic tradition that was painfully struggling toward maturity in the very period when *The Suppliants* was first performed. This anachronism, like the even more startling anachronisms in the latter part of *The Eumenides*, is a reminder of the extent to which Aeschylus' plays, despite the ancient mythological idiom in which they are expressed, were engaged with the momentous political events of their time, and with all the social and intellectual changes that those events implied.

The constitutional dimension of our play was not noticed by the professional classicists, so far as I can discover, until after the middle of the nineteenth century. It did not, however, escape the notice of another engaged poet, John Milton, two centuries before then. He discusses it at some length in his fierce defense of parliamentary government against a servile proponent of the Divine Right of Kings, in the *Pro Populo Anglicano Defensio* of 1651 (his views on the political lesson of *The Suppliants* may be read in the Columbia edition of his complete works, vol. 7, pp. 307–10). The poet who was living through the Periclean revolution seems to have spoken directly across the centuries to Oliver Cromwell's Latin Secretary at a crucial moment in the formation of modern European and American democracy. That is how the greater of the Greek classics have always tended to work, at least in those epochs when they have been treated seriously and not as mere schoolbooks. Conceived in life, they have begotten life.

Before we proceed to the remaining plays of the second group it may be well to recapitulate the main themes that have emerged from *The Suppliants* and from the remains of the tetralogy to which it belonged. They are: the confrontation between male and female at all levels of the universe; the idea of a movement from violence toward a peaceful and creative concord, epitomized in the phrase "release from sorrow"; Zeus and his ambiguous nature; parallel to that ambiguity, the ambiguity in the character of the Danaid maidens; and the political upheaval in contemporary Athens. It may be said in advance that all these phenomena will be found to recur in the *Oresteia* or in the Prometheus plays or in both.

Oresteia: Agamemnon

The *Oresteia* is an exemplary trinity. Simultaneously, it is both three, for each of its component plays can be, and often has been, staged as a separate artistic unit; and it is one, for there can be no comprehension of its full beauty and profundity until it is perceived as a unity. To stage *Agamemnon* on its own makes rather less sense than to perform the first movement of a Beethoven symphony on its own. The leading themes of the *Oresteia* are, it is true, introduced in *Agamemnon*, but in a confused and confusing way, for this play depicts a world in moral chaos, a world in which there seem to be no fixed principles left to hold on to. Those themes are clarified and separated out in *The Libation-Bearers*, but under conditions of at least equal hopelessness. The process of clarification, and the hopelessness too, persist into *The Eumenides*. Only in

the last third of the last play are the themes finally orches-
trated—into a hymn of joy that is no less startling in this
context of tragedy than the intrusion of the human voice into
an orchestra is in the last movement of the Ninth Symphony.

Correspondingly, as we should by now have come to
expect of Aeschylus, the overall movement in this trilogy is
from poetry heard to drama seen. *Agamemnon* is poetry heard
for almost its entire length. Although it is far and away the
longest of Aeschylus' surviving plays, the significant events
that take place during its dramatic present can be described
in a single sentence: The overlord of the Greeks, Agamemnon, returning from the Trojan War to his palace in Argos, is
there murdered by his wife Clytaemnestra, abetted by her
lover, Aegisthus. Yet not only does the central incident of the
murder occur offstage, out of the audience's sight (throughout
Attic tragedy, with only a few partial exceptions, the civilized
convention persists that acts of violence must not be represented onstage), it is even unfocused, as it were, in time; for
it is seen and described by the seeress Cassandra some minutes before it actually happens (lines 1100–35, compare 1223–
46). That blurring of edges is in fact characteristic of the whole
drama. *Agamemnon* is a play of ambiguities; and in Aeschylus
ambiguity is primarily the domain of the spoken word.

By far the greatest part of the play is devoted to the
pursuit of the two interlinked questions: what were the sequences of events that led up to the murder? And on whose
side did justice lie? As far as line 781, the speaking and the
singing are preoccupied with a meditation on the guilt incurred in the Trojan War. We hear of the guilt of Paris, who
lured Helen away from her husband, Menelaus, to live with
him in Troy; of Menelaus and his elder brother Agamemnon,
who did not shrink from causing a terrible war in order to
bring one woman home; but above all of Agamemnon him-

self, who cruelly sacrificed his and Clytaemnestra's daughter Iphigenia to obtain a fair wind for the Greek armada as it waited to set out, and then, after finally conquering Troy, simply obliterated it—people, walls, altars, temples, the very seeds that lay hidden beneath its soil (lines 525–28). By the moment of Agamemnon's triumphal entrance into the theater at line 782, he appears about as guilty as a man could be— guilty as a commander and guilty as a father and husband. Yet a further token of his guilt is embodied in the seeress Cassandra, who rides in his procession; she is not only a representative of the many Trojan women who were enslaved after the sack, but she has also been taken by Agamemnon as his mistress. On her, in fact, hinges the transition to the second sequence of causes that lead to Agamemnon's murder. In her superb scene from line 1072 to line 1330, she penetrates with her second sight into both the past and future horrors that lie within the palace walls, and in so doing reveals a side of Clytaemnestra that up to now has been hinted at only in riddles: on Clytaemnestra too lies guilt, for what she has done and for what she is about to do. This technique, which we tentatively remarked on in discussing the Danaids, of representing a character in contradictory aspects and revealing only gradually which is the true face, is richly exploited throughout the *Oresteia*; probably the most spectacular example will be found toward its end, in Aeschylus' handling of the Furies in *The Eumenides.*

From the Cassandra scene onward, the play's emphasis shifts to the causes, near and remote, that led Clytaemnestra to her act of murder. Near is her adulterous love affair, during Agamemnon's long absence, with his cousin Aegisthus. Remote was a vendetta that had begun in the preceding generation. Atreus (father of Agamemnon and Menelaus) and his brother Thyestes had long feuded over the lordship of Argos.

At last Atreus invited Thyestes into the palace—the same palace in front of which *Agamemnon* is set—on the pretense of a reconciliation. At the welcoming feast he fed the flesh of Thyestes' own butchered children to him. On discovering what the food was, Thyestes pronounced a great curse on the entire family. Atreus then drove him into exile, and with him the only one of his children who had escaped the butchery, an infant, Aegisthus. And none other than Aegisthus is the last character to make an entrance in *Agamemnon*. His epiphany culminates visually the meditation on the second sequence of crimes, very much as Agamemnon's epiphany, earlier, had culminated the meditation on the first.

The search for causes and justifications which thus dominated the play naturally entails a vast sweep outward and backward from the dramatic place and dramatic time at which *Agamemnon* is set. If the audience was to assess the true moral implications of the murder, it would ideally need to be transported to prewar Troy as it welcomed Helen into the city, for instance, or to the Argive palace at the moment when the smiling Atreus watched the meal being set before his brother. That kind of free movement through time and space, or something very close to it, was long after to be conferred on dramatists by the invention of cinematography. But already Aeschylus' verbal poetry, if rightly listened to, is capable of producing very nearly the same effects; and in *Agamemnon*, by every reader's experience, his verbal poetry reaches its supreme heights. We have already mentioned one or two examples of that poetry's power to transport the spectator just beyond the physical limits of the stage setting: the Shield Scene in *The Seven Against Thebes* and Danaus' description of the arrival of the Egyptian squadron in *The Suppliants*. In *Agamemnon*, however, it soars effortlessly from the palace at Argos, over the mountains to the east, across the Aegean sea to

the Hellespont and Troy, bringing back word-pictures so vivid
that they fix themselves in the mind's eye scarcely less than
in the ear. One remembers as clearly as if they had been
physically staged the preparations for the sacrifice of Iphigenia, described entirely in song in the latter part of the opening chorus (lines 223–47)—not least, perhaps, the appalling
detail of the piteous look in the little girl's eyes during her
last moments of life, after Agamemnon had ordered his attendants to gag her; or Clytaemnestra's pictures of Troy in
the dawn light immediately after its fall (lines 320–37): the
crude disharmony of voices as the conquered wail and the
conquerors cry out for joy; the pathetic little heaps formed by
the living Trojan young who have fallen across the corpses of
the old; and the Greek soldiers jostling to find a breakfast and
a good billet now that the night's work is over. Likewise one
remembers the Herald's account of the common soldier's life
in the Greek forward outposts during the long siege (lines
558–66), so much closer to the eternal realities of military life
than anything to be found in Homer: the ever-present damp,
the rotting uniforms, the lice, the "bird-killing cold" of winter,
and the murderous heat of the summer days, when the Hellespont "Waveless and windless dozed in its noonday rest."

  Yet it is Helen, perhaps, who abides most clearly in one's
memory after a reading of *Agamemnon*, even though she never
physically appears in the play. Here are two glimpses of her,
and of what she meant. In the choral passage from line 403
to line 426 we are told how Menelaus felt after she had left
him; lines 414–26 run somewhat like this:

> Yearning for a woman,
> A woman over sea,
> He shall think the ghost of her
> Is true master in his house.

The charm of statues carved in her perfect form
Shall rouse his hate. When the living eyes are lost,
Any love is ended.

Sad fancies shining out of dreams
Are about him still, to offer hollow joy.
He touches her?
—Straightway the vision flitting through his arms
Is gone, lightly on wings down the trails of sleep.

And here is a vision of Helen on her arrival at Troy (lines 737–42):

When she first came, I should call her
The thought of peace at sea when the winds are down,
Gentle arrow of the eyes,
Stingheart flower of love!

In relatively few lyric lines (one should add 681–749 and 1455–60 to what I have quoted above), Aeschylus creates out of words alone a Helen of Troy quite as lovely and as demonic as most of the Helens who have actually walked on the stage in later dramas. But these passages have not been composed just as virtuoso feats to be admired in passing, brilliant though they are. Helen is an integral part of the moral texture of *Agamemnon*. We must stand in her magnificent presence for a while if we are to comprehend the full cause and significance of the king's murder. And, through Aeschylus' poetry, we do so stand.

Another equally important aspect of Aeschylus' art in *Agamemnon* (and indeed, in this case, in the *Oresteia* as a whole) may be introduced through the play's prologue. The opening words of any Aeschylean drama, but above all of this one, need to be listened to with the same concentration as that with which one listens to the first measures of a Bach

fugue. The speech that the weary Watchman delivers in the
pre-dawn darkness from the roof of Agamemnon's palace em-
bodies many themes that will be developed in surprising ways
from one end of the trilogy to the other, some of them even
emerging into visible form. In the following translation of *Agamemnon* 1–22, I have italicized the most significant of those
themes:

> I ask the Gods *deliverance from these pains*,
> This watching; for a whole year's length I have lain
> Muzzle to paws, doglike, on the Atreids' roof,
> Learning to know the parliament of night—
> Those stars who bring the seasons, cold and heat,
> Bright lords in splendor set against the sky.
>   And still I watch for the *signal of the light*,
> For the *glare of fire* to bring the news from Troy,
> Shouting her fall!
>   Those are my orders, issued
> By *a woman who plans in her male heart*, and waits.
> My bed is no bed, restless through the night
> And damp with dew. No *dreams* can visit there,
> For fear, not sleep, is all my company.
> I cannot ever firmly close my eyes.
>   Sometimes I think I'll sing or hum, to cure
> My sleepiness by the medicine of music—
> But then instead I weep, I mourn aloud
> For this house and its state; it is no longer
> Managed as excellently as it was of old.
>   Now come, happy *deliverance from pains*,
> The *fire in blackness* flaring its glad news!
>   [He gestures as if he has seen the beacon far
>   offstage.]
> Welcome, you *lamp of night shining as day!*

These lines, like the rest of the Watchman's speech, and indeed like much of *Agamemnon*, are of the stuff of nightmare. The shifting, contradictory imagery—light out of darkness, day out of night, the female with the male heart—are matched by shifting, contradictory emotions, hope and terror, the urge to sing that melts into weeping. Opening and closing the passage that precedes the Watchman's sighting of the beacon is a prayer for deliverance from pains. Eventually that will be understood, in fact, to have struck the keynote for the entire trilogy, but not until the last few minutes of its performance. In the interim, again in nightmare fashion, deliverance will retreat further and further with each step the characters seem to take toward it. The light the simple Watchman believes to herald it will soon prove to be more terrifying than the darkness out of which it issued, for it bears not only the news of victory at Troy but also a signal to the waiting Queen Clytaemnestra that the time has arrived to prepare for murder. Several times the characters who appear later in *Agamemnon* will salute the day, or the light, or Justice (*Dikē*), or all three, as if the speaker's cause has been finally vindicated and the slate of ancient crime and suffering has been wiped clean. "Agamemnon comes," says the Herald (lines 521–26), "bringing us light in our night-time. . . . Greet him, who has dug Troy into the ground with the pick-axe of Justice-bearing Zeus!" When Agamemnon himself arrives, his first words are (lines 810–14): "First it is justice to address Argos and the Gods who live in her, who helped me to come home, and to exact just punishment from the city of Priam; for the Gods heard my unspoken pleas for justice. . . ." After the murder has been done, Clytaemnestra cries to the Chorus (lines 1432–36): "Now, by the justice that has been fulfilled for my daughter [Iphigenia], I swear to you that my expectation does not tread within Fear's palace, so long as I have Aegisthus like a blazing fire upon my hearth." And when Aegisthus finally shows himself upon the stage, his first line is (1577): "O kindly light of justice-bearing day!"

That is only one image-cluster of many that run through the trilogy, and only one illustration of the moral confusion that reigns in *Agamemnon*. Each party in turn claims that justice is on his or her side and that the light shines for him or her alone. But for Agamemnon and the Herald, as for Clytaemnestra and Aegisthus, light and justice will prove to be no more than will-o'-the-wisps, phantoms that, like the dream of Helen, will soon be off and away, "lightly on wings down the trails of sleep." No certainties are left in the world, except the certainty that crime means more crime. As the Chorus sings toward the end of the great scene (1412–1576) in which they and Clytaemnestra together review all the possible causes and justifications of the murder, both human and divine,

> It is a losing battle to decide,
> For ravaged ravages again,
> And murderer pays murder's price.

Even the two visual tableaux that *Agamemnon* contains, although among the most famous dramatic spectacles in Greek tragedy, do not solve any mysteries in the way that Aeschylean tableaux are elsewhere apt to do. Rather, they make plain to the eye once and for all the reality, first of Agamemnon's guilt, then of Clytaemnestra's. Taken as a responding pair, as they are surely designed to be, they simply emphasize the moral dilemma around which the play is built. In the episode that has come to be known as the Tapestry Scene (lines 905–74), where Clytaemnestra tempts Agamemnon not to set his foot on this common earth but to approach the palace over purple cloths that she has had her servants

lay from the chariot to the palace door, the arrogance and folly
in the heart of Troy's conqueror are given magnificent external expression. Knowing as he well does that such an honor
should be reserved for the gods alone, he at last lets himself
be persuaded to walk that purple path and to go through the
door to his eventual death. For a moment, the opening in the
skēnē with its protruding purple tongue may remind us of the
Hell-Mouth in a mediaeval mystery play; and that indeed is
very close to its meaning here. The second great tableau occurs abruptly at line 1372, where that same palace door
swings open to reveal Clytaemnestra standing over her husband's corpse. The body lies in a silver bath (as is shown by
lines 1539–40), still wrapped in the folds of the great cloth in
which she entangled him before stabbing him (lines 1382–84,
1492, 1580). Visible also is the body of the slaughtered Cassandra (line 1440). The corpses can be seen throughout Clytaemnestra's inconclusive debate with the Chorus about the
causes of the murder, and are still there for Aegisthus to gloat
over at his entrance (lines 1581–82). No doubt they remain on
view until the end of the play, mute witnesses to Clytaemnestra's crime.

Agamemnon then, brings us no certainties, religious or
moral or even emotional—the manic-depressive swings of
mood that we noted already in the Watchman are experienced
also, for instance, by the Chorus (lines 99–103 offer a striking
example). No certainties; only, here and there, flareups of
intuition into truths which will be slowly justified in practice
as the trilogy unfolds. One such intuitional flareup, it seems
to me, is the passage 160–83, which is probably the most
famous song that Aeschylus ever composed. In modern times
it has come to be referred to, almost as if it were an independent poem, as the "Hymn to Zeus," and indeed at a first

hearing it may well appear to have little enough to do with its immediate context in the Chorus's great opening chant and song (lines 40–257, the longest uninterrupted choral utterance in Attic tragedy). As a whole, that chant and song are devoted to a vision of the preliminaries to the sailing of the expedition to Troy. The Chorus recalls (lines 104–59) the omen of the pair of eagles feasting on a pregnant hare, which the army-seer Calchas interpreted—and this is characteristic of the mood of the entire play—as simultaneously favorable and terrible: in the knot of writhing creatures he sees that Agamemnon and Menelaus will succeed in annihilating Troy, but that this act may bring upon them the anger of the goddess of all natural life, Artemis. The second major episode of the song (lines 184–257) lyrically narrates the immediate result of her anger: she caused contrary winds to blow where the fleet was moored at Aulis, and would not let it sail until Agamemnon sacrificed his own daughter to her. Interposed between these two ominous narratives, like a desperate cry for help out of the moral abyss, is the Hymn to Zeus.

The Zeus invoked here, like the second of the two facets of Zeus recognized in *The Suppliants* (see above, pp. 105–07), is a mysterious being of immense power. The Chorus is not even sure of his right name (lines 160–62); it only knows, like the Danaid chorus, that he is its sole hope of release from sorrow. For this is the God who has (lines 176–83)

> Brought human beings on the road to wisdom
> By setting firm this law:
> *Through suffering, learning!*
> At the heart's gate, even in sleep,
> Agony of remembered pain
> Falls drop by drop, and even to the unwilling
> Come wisdom and restraint.

> And do the Spirits who sit at the august helm
> Through violence show their kindness?

Since Byzantine times this intuition of a Zeus who guides mankind to righteousness through chastisement has reminded commentators of the message of the Old Testament. But even while we wonder at that resemblance, it is important to bear in mind certain differences too. First, taken in its dramatic context this passage is not to be understood (as it often seems to be) as Aeschylus' personal statement of a creed guaranteed by divine revelation. It is a point of view expressed by the old men of the Chorus—a hope, which they do not try to justify either by revelation or by experience. Second, this Zeus, like the transcendent Zeus invoked by the Danaids and unlike the God of the Old Testament, has a past behind him—a violent mythological past, which is alluded to in the second of the hymn's three stanzas. He wrestled down the previous lord of the universe, his own father, Kronos, who himself had dethroned *his* father, Ouranos; Heaven too has once known the chaos of the vendetta, just as humanity knows it now, at the dramatic time of *Agamemnon*. For the interpreter of the art of the *Oresteia*, the main significance of the Hymn to Zeus is that, at this early and desperate stage of the story, it introduces the ideas that human beings may *learn*, even at the cost of great agony, and that even the gods may, if not change, at least ultimately reveal a different face. Both ideas are in fact eventually realized in the progress of the trilogy, as is the Watchman's prayer for "deliverance from pains." The technique is basically the same as that which we have already witnessed in *The Persians*, where the elders' intuition into the laws of the archaic universe, expressed in their opening song, is only later corroborated by actual events; the difference is that the time-lapse between intuition and corroboration is far longer in the *Oresteia*, on account of its far greater scale.

Less generally noticed than the Hymn to Zeus, but perhaps no less marvelous an example of this technique, is another premonitory passage that occurs later in *Agamemnon*. At lines 1372–98 Clytaemnestra, standing over the two corpses, recalls moment by moment not merely the murder of Agamemnon but also her sensations as she committed it. Here is an attempt to render the culminating lines of that speech (1384–92):

> I strike him twice, and in a double scream
> He lets his limbs collapse. As he lies there,
> I throw in a third stab, to carry down
> My vow to Zeus our Savior under Earth
> —Zeus, Savior of corpses! So he falls
> And speeds away the spirit of his being,
> And puffing out a sudden spurt of gore
> Hits me with a dark shower of blood-red rain
> —And I rejoice, just as the seeded fields
> Delight in the liquid joy bestowed by heaven
> At the childbearing of the buds in spring!

This speech is riddled with blasphemy. Zeus in his aspect of Savior or Preserver, *Sōtēr*, was the deity to whom the Greeks customarily poured the third of the three ritual wine libations that opened a festive drinking-party or *symposion*. Here Clytaemnestra tauntingly transforms Zeus into his ghastly counterpart, Hades, lord of the dead (here one may well recall the blasphemous threat of the Danaids in *Suppliants* 154–75), and her libation is offered not in wine but in blood. But the image expressed in the last four lines quoted, the image that crossed her mind as Agamemnon's blood spurted over her, seems to imply the worst blasphemy of all. It is evidently a perversion

of the primaeval myth of the mating of Heaven and Earth in
the spring rains, which we heard from the mouth of Aphrodite in *The Danaides* (see above, p. 102). In that myth the
primal Male came together with the primal Female in the mutual joy of creation. Clytaemnestra, however, after that third
and wanton blow, seems to have cast Agamemnon in the role
of Heaven and herself in the role of Earth, while the spurt of
blood stood for the gentle falling of the rain/semen; she transformed the ancient world's supreme symbol of love between
the sexes into her own supreme symbol of hatred. In the
moment of murdering her husband, she intuited something
more terrifying even than murder: a universe divided by open
war between the male and the female. That intuition will become closer and closer to reality—onstage reality—in the
course of *The Libation-Bearers* and *The Eumenides*.

Oresteia: The Libation-Bearers

On the face of it, *The Libation-Bearers* might seem to be a
revenge-play of the type quite familiar in the later European
dramatic tradition. Students have often compared it to *Hamlet*,
and indeed one will notice some fascinating resemblances between the two plays. Even more interesting, however, are the
differences between the two playwrights' treatments of the
theme of the prince who avenges his father's murder. Just one
of those differences may be mentioned here, but that one
alone will illuminate the uniqueness of Aeschylean tragedy
by comparison with any tragedy that was to come. Hamlet
proceeds to his revenge through a long-protracted agony of
internal conflict. Orestes, having once reunited himself with
his sister and secured the support of his dead father's spirit,
proceeds to *his* revenge with swift and relentless efficiency;
only after the murder does his personality fall apart, and then

because it is violently invaded by a force from outside. Only then, also, does it begin to appear that in *The Libation-Bearers* we have been witnessing not merely an individual human being's act of vengeance, but the drawing of the lines in a cosmic conflict.

The action of the play, quite unlike that of *Agamemnon*, lies almost entirely in the dramatic here and now. There are few of those wide sweeps into distant places and the past on the wings of verbal poetry. Indeed, all the significant incidents in this plot which tragic convention permitted to be enacted onstage—that is, all except the actual murders—take place before the audience's eyes. It is in this respect (but perhaps, on reflection, one may think *only* in this respect) that *The Libation-Bearers* anticipates the effects of drama as drama has been understood from Sophocles onward more than any play of Aeschylus that we have seen so far. Especially in the scenes from line 652 (where Orestes presents himself at the palace door) until the end, the stage action moves as fast and as excitingly as it does in any modern thriller-play. I shall review *The Libation-Bearers* first in that strictly dramatic aspect. After that, I shall explore the poetic means by which Aeschylus, as the human revenge-story progresses, gradually clarifies the confused themes announced in *Agamemnon* and simultaneously prepares for the ultimate clarifications of *The Eumenides*.

This is how the revenge for Agamemnon's murder is brought about on the human plane: Orestes, under stringent orders from Apollo to execute that revenge (lines 269–305), returns to Argos from the Delphic territory of Phocis, to which his mother Clytaemnestra had sent him long ago, before the murder. With him is his Phocian friend, Pylades, a silent presence throughout except at lines 900–02, where he intervenes at a climactic moment almost with the voice of the Delphic

Apollo himself; but he is a constant visual reminder of Apollo's commitment to the vengeance. Orestes' first action is to pay homage at Agamemnon's tomb (represented by a mound in the center of the *orchēstra*?), laying on it a lock of his hair as an offering due to Inachus, the river-god of his native land, and another lock in mourning for Agamemnon. His devotions are interrupted by the entrance of his sister Electra and the Chorus, consisting of captive women, who are also bringing offerings to the tomb in the form of libations. The two men withdraw out of sight of the procession, while the grim tomb-ritual takes its course. It soon appears from the women's words that Clytaemnestra has ordered these belated rites to be observed as the result of an ominous dream (lines 32–46).

Just after Electra has poured the libations at the tomb-mound, she notices the lock and the footprints left there by Orestes and concludes from the resemblances to her own hair and feet that they must be his. At that point Orestes steps forward and finally convinces her of his identity by showing her another token—a piece of cloth that he carries woven by Electra in her childhood long ago. The sheer unrealism of this recognition scene, by any ordinary standards of logic, has been noted by Aeschylus' critics ever since Euripides, who less than half a century later exposed it with wicked humor in his *Electra* (lines 508–45 of that play). It is yet another reminder of the gulf that separates Aeschylus from any later tragedian. One cannot enforce ordinary realistic standards on these characters of his, who are both more and less than ordinary individuals, who exist on the borderline between life as we know it and a mythical, demonic world. In that world, as in a fairy-tale or a nightmare, the incongruous or the impossible may make better sense than any petty realities, as symbols of a deeper intuited truth. Of course, it is implausible that a sister, by comparing an unknown lock of hair and a set of footprints with her own hair and feet, should know instantly that they belong to her brother and no one else in the world; while obviously any stranger, even an enemy bent on betraying Electra, might somehow have acquired that piece of weaving. Yet there could hardly be any more powerful symbols than those for their bond as sister and brother, two alone against the wide world. In evaluating this and many other scenes in Aeschylus, we might do better to apply the criteria of surrealism than those of realism.

There remains a third family member who must be drawn into the reunion before the vengeance can proceed. It is, again, characteristic of the Aeschylean vision that Orestes, Electra, and the Chorus have still to exert all their powers in order to bring the spirit of Agamemnon to their aid from the recesses of Earth. They do so by means of a tremendous chant, dance, and song around the funeral mound (lines 306–478), which is the most elaborately composed operatic scene in Aeschylus' surviving work and, as such, unfortunately, the most difficult to translate into two-dimensional English verse, as it were; here more than anywhere the reader needs imaginatively to bring the flat text up into its original rhythm, melody, and spectacle. The chanting and singing lead into an antiphony in unaccompanied spoken verse between Orestes and Electra (lines 479–509), in which their incantation rises to a desperate urgency, as if the sheer force of words might compel the dead king out of his grave:

> *Orestes:* Send up, O Earth, my father to watch over this battle!
> *Electra:* And grant, Persephone, victory's lovely form! . . .
> *Orestes:* My father, are you now waking at this tale of your dishonor?
> *Electra:* Are you now raising up your much-loved head?

Anyone who had watched *The Persians* fourteen years earlier might well have been in fearful suspense by this point: would the ghastly figure of the murdered man now slowly rise out of the mound, as the serene ghost of Darius had risen after a similar but in fact much shorter tomb-ritual? But here Aeschylus deludes our expectations; this is not yet the time in the trilogy for the supernatural powers to be manifested to the eye, only for them to press closer and closer against the flimsy curtain which separates them from living humanity.

After the ritual is over, Orestes is further emboldened by the Chorus's description of the nightmare that had impelled Clytaemnestra to send the procession to the tomb (lines 514–22): the dread vision of a snake to which she gave suck and which in that process bit into her breast, drawing blood along with the mother's milk. Thus, now triply armed with the protection of Apollo, the power of his father's spirit, and the portent that has emerged out of the darkness of his mother's mind, Orestes is at last ready to lay his plans for the murder, as he does in lines 555–84. He and his silent companion, Pylades, leave the scene through one of the side passages, while Electra withdraws into the palace. The theatral area is left to the Chorus, which now sings that ode, part of which was quoted earlier, on the destructive powers that lie within the human heart, and especially within the heart of Woman (above, pp. 10–11).

The action that follows the central ode moves before our eyes with remarkable speed until the end of the play. Even the sung and chanted interventions of the Chorus are no longer the lengthy, far-ranging lyric meditations to which we have been used so far in Aeschylus' work, but relatively short and businesslike, being directly involved with the action at hand; the song at lines 783–837, for instance, has practically the effect of a war-dance, putting heart into Orestes for the kill. Orestes, for his part, wastes very little time. At line 652 he and Pylades, both in the disguise of Phocian travelers, appear at the palace door, to which the focus of the play's action now shifts from the tomb-mound. (Aeschylus was no slave to what was later called "the Unity of Place": a similar shift of focus, this time *to* a tomb, has already been seen in *The Persians,* and very much more drastic ones will occur in *The Eumenides.*) They are greeted by Clytaemnestra in person, whom Orestes persuades by a plausible story that he, Orestes, has lately died in his Phocian exile. She has the apparent strangers conducted into the men's quarters of the palace, and herself withdraws in order to see that her lord, Aegisthus, is informed of the news.

But Clytaemnestra's caution and resourcefulness have not deserted her, even when to all appearances the last possible threat to her and Aegisthus' security has been removed by Orestes' death. This we learn indirectly from the next person to enter, the old slave-woman Cilissa, who nursed Orestes in his infancy. Clytaemnestra, she says, has sent her out to tell Aegisthus to come and hear the strangers' story, adding the instruction that he must come not alone but with his bodyguard. The Chorus narrowly saves the conspirators from total failure there and then by persuading the innocent old woman to leave out the second part of that message. The Cilissa scene (lines 734–82) illustrates a dimension of Aeschylus' art that appears in the *Oresteia* alone of his extant plays: its capacity to characterize the common man with sympathy and even tenderness. The speeches of the Watchman and the Herald in *Agamemnon* offer many hints of this quite unexpected side of our poet—unexpected, that is, to anyone who has not read the fragments and who has approached the extant plays, as we have done, in chronological order (contrast, for instance, the speeches of the Messengers in *The Persians* and *The Seven*

Against Thebes). But it is Cilissa who stands out from this point of view. Amid the schemings, the hypocrisies, and the demonic passions of the princes, which are richly exemplified in the scenes on either side of this one, she stands desolated by simple, unaffected sorrow at the news of Orestes' supposed death. She can see the hero only as the baby whom she loved with all her heart, even though his screams troubled her nights, and though his soiled clothing cost her endless labor at the washtub (lines 748–63).

Thus Aegisthus arrives without any attendants and unsuspectingly enters the door of the men's quarters. His murder follows after a very short interval, being signaled to the audience by a scream offstage (line 869; one does not miss the symmetry between the effects here and those at the moment of Agamemnon's murder). One of his servants rushes out to summon Clytaemnestra, who presently enters, to be faced by Orestes and Pylades. At this culmination of his plot Orestes falters only for one moment, and that is when his mother points to the breast with which she suckled him as an infant and appeals to him to revere it. Confronted in this most elemental way with the full meaning of what he has set out to do, he turns to Pylades for advice; and Pylades speaks for the first and only time in the play (lines 900–02), sternly reminding him of his obligation to Apollo's oracle and to the gods. There is an end to hesitation: step by step, it seems, to the accompaniment of a line-by-line interchange between them (lines 908–28), the son forces the mother back through the palace door. During that drawn-out retreat toward inevitable death she threatens him with a mother's curse, expressing it in line 924 in the shape of a riddling warning:

Look now, beware of your mother's spiteful hounds!

Their disappearance, followed by Pylades, into that

doom-laden palace door is followed by a triumph-song from the Chorus. Then, at line 973, the door swings open again to display Orestes, with Pylades, standing over the corpses of Clytaemnestra and Aegisthus. The awesome tableau, of course, corresponds to the tableau revealed at *Agamemnon* 1372 and results, for the moment, in a sense of completed symmetry, a sense of an ending. The clear message to the audience's eyes, as well as to its mind, is that the age-old law of retaliation has been fulfilled, and the family vendetta has reached the point where no human avengers are left. But the final scene of *The Libation-Bearers* (lines 973–1076) will transform all. Before proceeding to it, however, it will be well to turn for a while from the surface action of the play to consider the means by which Aeschylus has all along been unobtrusively leading up to that last and most terrible revelation.

The mood of *The Libation-Bearers* is visually set from the first by the black costumes in which the Chorus members are dressed (line 11). Indeed, from their entrance until very near the end of the *Oresteia* as whole (as will be seen later), the theater is dominated by the great black rectangle composed by the successive choruses of women and of Furies. Morally, too, the trilogy is progressing ever deeper into blackness. Here and there the verbal imagery, as in *Agamemnon*, offers a flare of light; but, also as in *Agamemnon*, the light's message will prove a delusion. The instances are worth recalling before we proceed to that final scene of our play. On a probable reading of the Greek text, Electra at line 131 begs the dead Agamemnon to "kindle Orestes as a light in our house"; just before Aegisthus' murder the Chorus prays (lines 808–10) that "the light of Freedom may look on Orestes," showing its "kindly eyes from out the veil of darkness"; and in its song during Clytaemnestra's murder the refrain is twice heard, "the light is here to see!" As with light, so with justice, which

was so often associated with it in *Agamemnon*. Throughout
our play the murder of Clytaemnestra is represented by the
conspirators as the fulfillment of justice. Thus, early on, Electra prays at the tomb (line 144) "that those who killed may
die through justice in return," and the Chorus, in the song
during Clytaemnestra's murder that was just quoted, proclaims (lines 948–51) that Justice, the daughter of Zeus,
"breathing mortal rage against our enemies," has laid her
hand on that of Orestes in this struggle.

On the whole, therefore, the idea of justice which prevails
in *The Libation-Bearers* is no different from that which prevailed
in the previous play. It continues to be equated with the iron
law of retaliation, just as it was by the Herald, Agamemnon,
Clytaemnestra, and Aegisthus in turn, and its seeming fulfillment is still seen as the light of salvation. Where Orestes
and Electra differ from the actors of *Agamemnon*, in fact, is not
in their perception of justice, but in the spirit in which they
execute it. They show none of the cruel satisfaction with
which the Herald and Agamemnon spoke of the justice dealt
out to Troy, still less the unholy ecstasy which the king's murder inspired in Clytaemnestra and Aegisthus, Electra, indeed,
in the very speech at the tomb in which she prays for the
return and vengeance of Orestes, includes the prayer (lines
140–41): "and for myself, grant that I may be far more chaste
than my mother, and more pious in my acts." The brother
and sister seem to possess an intuition, still unformulated, of
a justice that transcends revenge. And yet the murder, the
murder of a mother by her son, must still be carried out.
Apollo, the Olympian deity of the light, has ordered it and
guaranteed Orestes his protection. Orestes' murdered father
has been summoned from the grave to his support. On three
levels of being—divine, human, and infernal—the male has
been aligning its forces to crush a woman—or is Clytaemnes-

tra to be thought of just as an individual woman? Remembering her perception of herself at the moment she stabbed her husband (above, p. 123), we may wonder. But not until the last scene of *The Libation-Bearers* is there any further hint that on her side, too, an array of powers is being lined up, this time female powers.

To return at last to that scene: the tableau revealed at line 973 is both a counterpart and a contrast to the tableau of *Agamemnon* 1372. Again the slayer stands over the slain, but Orestes is carrying the garlanded bough (line 1035) that proclaims him to be a suppliant of Apollo. Shortly afterward, in another of the magnificent visual gestures of the *Oresteia*, he has his attendants stretch out the great, still bloodstained cloth in which Agamemnon was entangled at his murder, and show it to the sunlight, as justification for his act. There is no triumph in his words: only, first, an almost hysterical condemnation of his mother's wickedness, then a realization (line 1017) of the depth of the pollution that he has incurred, then (line 1021) an admission that his mind is violently swerving beyond the bounds of sanity. He only has time, before madness strikes, to claim once more the patronage of Apollo, knowing that his only hope now is to reach the temple at Delphi and its "undying light of fire" (line 1037); yet once again in the trilogy the elusive light has flickered away into the far distance. Suddenly (line 1048) he lets out a great scream. Visible to him alone, the female supernatural powers are moving in on him; they appear to him as a swarm of Gorgon-like women, black-clothed, with snakes entangled in their hair and blood oozing from their eyes. As yet he can give them no name—neither he nor the audience, in fact, will be certain about that until well into the following play—but at least he can now solve the riddle that Clytaemnestra posed as she retreated to the palace door: "these are my mother's

spiteful hounds, clear to the eye" (line 1054; compare 924).
As he rushes from the scene to try to escape them, the
Chorus, unwittingly echoing the thought of the Watchman at
the very beginning of th trilogy, assure him that "Apollo will
set you free from these sorrows" (lines 1059–60). After he has
vanished, however, their feelings are less confident. In their
recessional chant they reflect on the interminability of blood-
feud. First came the banquet served by Atreus to Thyestes,
then the murder of Agamemnon, and now?

> Now for the third time has arrived from somewhere
> A Savior—or should I call him Doom?
> Where will it consummate,
> Where will it rest and fall asleep at last,
> The spirit of destruction?

Even the Chorus has seen at the last that the old justice
and the old light have failed. The vendetta has not ended. As
will be revealed more clearly in the final play of the *Oresteia*,
it is to continue on a vaster scale, involving the fundamental
powers in the universe and human life as we experience it:
the male and the female.

Oresteia: The Eumenides

The Eumenides stands to the rest of the *Oresteia* somewhat
as the epiphany of Darius in *The Persians* stands to all that has
gone before in that play. The supernatural takes visible shape,
and with that manifestation all doubts are dispelled. In its
light we can at last make sense of the mysteries in the human
story that has been told so far. But in *The Persians*, as we saw,
the divine epiphany occupied only a single episode, and it
revealed a static universe at peace with itself, its harmony
disturbed only by the transgression of mortal pride. The

epiphany of *The Eumenides* occupies an entire play, and it is a progressive revelation of a universe in the midst of violent change. The drama and its suspense continue, but they continue partly on to the divine plane. Almost from the first we are made to realize with the utmost clarity something that we may have surmised toward the end of *The Libation-Bearers* and something that Clytaemnestra had already intuited as she murdered Agamemnon: at stake in the human feud which has unfolded in the two earlier plays is nothing less than the relationship between male and female throughout the universe.

In the rapid succession of scenes at Delphi (lines 1–235), the representatives of the male and female divine forces appear before our eyes in bitter enmity with each other. And they are, indeed, only representatives. Apollo speaks with the voice of Zeus (this is stressed three times, at lines 19, 615–18, and 713), and hence of the Olympian patriarchy (line 618); the Furies invoke as their allies two of the oldest female deities in the cosmos—Night (lines 321–22, 416, 745, 792, 822, 845, 877) and Fate, alternatively referred to as the Fates (lines 172, 335, 392, 961). It is significant that in this play Aeschylus differs from all other recorded Greek genealogies of the gods by making the Furies the daughters of Night, who is Fate's sister (see lines 961–62). By so doing he both elevates their cosmic status and directly associates them with darkness; and indeed, darkness or blackness prove to be characteristic both of the Furies and of the feminine generally. The Furies' costumes are black (line 370; compare *Libation-Bearers* 1049), like those of the women in the Chorus of *The Libation-Bearers*, and line 52 may even imply that their masks and limbs are black also. They dwell in the darkness below earth (lines 72 and 395), in a gloom that knows no sunlight (line 396, compare 386–87). Athena, says Apollo, did not come to being "in the darkness of the womb" (line 665); on the other hand, as Orestes claims, Clytaemnestra's "thoughts were black" (459).

At last, then, the confused imagery of light and dark that has pervaded the trilogy since the Watchman's opening speech is, as it were, polarized and actually presented to the eye. Light (male, heavenly, patriarchal) is flatly opposed to darkness (female, earthly, matriarchal). So long as this rift endures there can be no hope of creation in any sense or at any level. The fruits of the earth will not grow, cattle will not multiply, neither families nor larger societies will hold together. All these consequences, as we shall see, are increasingly stressed in the latter half of *The Eumenides*. The universe is in peril of a state opposite to that envisaged in Aphrodite's picture of the ultimate sexual union in *The Danaides* (above, p. 102). In the *Oresteia*, it seems, as in that earlier trilogy on the fate of the Danaids, Aeschylus is still preoccupied with the human male-female relationship as a symbol that will illuminate the workings of the cosmos. Here, however, its symbolism takes on political, legal, and social dimensions as well. One of the most surprising features of *The Eumenides*, by comparison with any other Attic tragedy, is its direct involvement with the political situation existing in Athens at the time when the play was first produced. Until the end of the episodes at Delphi, the *Oresteia*'s action is laid in the practically timeless world of heroic saga. From the moment (line 235) at which the scene shifts to Athens, the drama homes in increasingly on the Athenian here and now. The Furies are made to appear, concurrently, less and less as insensate bloodhounds seeking the punishment of a matricide merely by instinctive reflex, and more and more as the upholders of an ancient tradition of family values, a tradition that to them represents justice, *dikē* (see their song in lines 490–565, and especially 508–16). It must be said, even perhaps at the cost of arousing a smile, that by the middle of *The Eumenides* the Furies are seen to be strict conservatives, in human as in cosmic politics. On the other hand, the Olympian representatives, first Apollo and then Athena, defend—the latter more moderately and intelligently than the former—a still perfectly recognizable liberal point of view: human and divine society can be changed by political means, and there may be times when this becomes necessary, even at great risk to inherited traditions of conduct.

The fundamental conflict in values represented by the two parties in *The Eumenides* has, of course, been a persistent feature of Western civilization ever since, and there have been (and will yet be, so long as that civilization endures) many times when it has shaken a social fabric to pieces, or come very close to doing so. One may think, for instance, of the sixteenth- and seventeenth-century wars of religion; or of the Vietnam years. But here above all, as we approach *The Eumenides*, it is pertinent to recall what was said in chapter 2 concerning the political and social transitions that were taking place during the last years of Aeschylus' life—the violent reform of the ancient court of Areopagus, the institution of the Periclean democracy (a process that was reaching its climax during the very year in which the *Oresteia* was first played), and the concurrent revolution in intellectual and religious, as well as political life. What makes this particular clash between the conservative and the liberal mentalities different is that it was the first such clash in recorded history—at least on this scale and with this variety of dimensions. The rift in Aeschylus' dramatic cosmos was paralleled by the rift in Aeschylus' city and perhaps—who knows?—the rift in his very soul and in the souls of his fellow citizens. *The Eumenides* seems to attempt both a diagnosis of and a remedy for what was then a new and fearsome disease of human society. That disease, now inveterate, remains fearsome; and Aeschylus' insights

into it, at that historical moment when it first struck our society with the abrupt force of plague, may still reward our
study.

But how, at this distance, can we penetrate to those insights? The difficulties are great. As was seen in the first two
chapters of this book, the drama of Aeschylus is unique (at
least in the Western world) in that, to the end, he worked in
and through the language, the shapes, and the symbolism of
the ancient mythology in all their dreamlike strangeness; and
yet through that very medium he tried to come to grips with
the great fifth-century transition from the very old ways of
thinking to the very new. We cannot expect from that medium, as perhaps too many modern commentators and students have expected, a logical exposition of the problems and
solutions. What we can reasonably expect—and what, I think,
we get, above all in *The Eumenides*—is an almost absurdist
drama, in which the events are superficially incongruous or
incredible to the philosophically trained mind, but in which
the symbolism pierces home to truth. One example of a scene
composed in that mode, the recognition between Orestes and
Electra, was singled out for discussion above (pp. 126–27). In
The Eumenides we have before us an entire play so composed.
Before considering its course, we may do well to recall some
of the words of Artaud that were quoted at the end of
chapter 1:

> Manikins, enormous masks, objects of strange propor-
> tions, will appear with the same sanction as verbal im-
> ages.

> The Theater of Cruelty will choose subjects and themes
> corresponding to the agitation and unrest characteristic
> of our epoch. . . . It will cause not only the recto but the
> verso of the mind to play its part; the reality of imagi-

nation and dreams will appear there on an equal footing
with life.

The Eumenides falls into three main movements, of which
the first (lines 1–234) is set before the door of Apollo's temple
at Delphi. A series of brief scenes expounds the contrast between the radiant Olympian god and the black, bestial creatures which have swarmed out of the depths of the earth into
his sanctuary. The serenity of the Priestess' opening prayer
to the gods and landscape of Delphi (significantly, in view of
the play's outcome, it begins with Earth and ends with "Zeus
the Highest") stands in shocking contrast to the second half
of her speech, where she tries to describe the vision that
awaited her after her solemn entrance into the temple at line
34. Her report makes it clear that for Orestes the light has
once more failed, even Apollo's "undying light of fire." Even
as he sits at the very center of Apollo-worship, his hands are
still, magically, dripping with Clytaemnestra's blood, and he
is encircled by sleeping female creatures whose horrific nature
the priestess can only report in a breathless series of rejected
comparisons: these things are women but not women, Gorgons but not Gorgons, Harpies but not Harpies. Something
worse even than the worst horrors created by the ancient
mythic imagination has crept out of the pit.

After the exit of the Priestess, the divine adversaries and
their human protégés are brought in turn before our eyes.
First Orestes enters from the temple accompanied by Apollo,
who tells him that he must now wander over land and sea,
pursued by the Furies, until he comes to Athens. There he is
to embrace Athena's image, and there jurors, dikastai, will be
found to try his case. Thus, says Apollo (lines 82–83), "I shall
find ways utterly to deliver you from these pains"; again we
hear an echo of the phrase used by the Watchman at the

opening of the trilogy. After the god and the man have left the scene, it is the turn of the female party. In one of his most superb imaginative strokes Aeschylus introduces the murdered Clytaemnestra, still showing the gashes that Orestes inflicted on her, not just as a ghost but as the dream of a ghost, angrily appealing to her patrons, the Furies, rousing them from the depths of their sleep. Here yet another motif that has persisted throughout the *Oresteia* seems to reach its climax; its first, muted introduction may be sought in the Watchman's insistence that *his* bed is not visited by dreams.

How this scene was staged is uncertain, but I would follow those who guess that the figure of the dream-ghost appears at the open door of the temple, calling to the Furies still unseen within, then vanishes as they awaken and make their way out one by one into the view of the spectators. However it was staged their epiphany must have been sensational. Characteristically, Aeschylus had built up the suspense and mystery by verbal means, step by step from Clytaemnestra's riddling threat in *The Libation-Bearers* (line 924), through the vision seen by the crazed Orestes at the end of the same play, to the description by the bewildred Priestess as she reentered from the polluted shrine; now, and only now, appeared the visible reality. The story in the anonymous ancient Greek *Life of Aeschylus* that through this apparition the poet "so shocked the people that the children fainted away, and there were miscarriages," may not be literally true (for the *Life* is a late and reckless compilation from all kinds of sources, reliable and the reverse), but it seems very well invented on the basis of the text.

Now that the divine adversaries have been manifested separately, the time has arrived for their confrontation in the last of the scenes at Delphi (lines 179–231), where the resplendent Apollo threatens the black and hideous Furies with his golden bow. This tableau may be said to mark the lowest point of despair in the *Oresteia*; both the vision and the words that accompany it indicate a hopeless and irreconcilable enmity between the opposed divine forces who for the present control events. Before passing on from that dread vision to the central movement of *The Eumenides* (lines 235–777), we should pause to consider a question that is perhaps not asked often enough either in practical living or in the criticism of Aeschylus: *how are debates on vital issues actually won?* Between adversaries opposed on grounds of deeply felt principle, unfortunately for humanity, simple reasoning rarely seems to achieve much—no more than simple arithmetic can achieve in a debate on moral values, for instance. In such matters conversion to another's point of view, on the rare occasions when it occurs, is rather a process of *turning* (as is implied in the etymology of the word *conversion*), a turning of the total personality of each party toward that of the other in such a way as to reveal previously unrecognized compatible qualities; and this difficult process is apt to be induced by the heavy stress of changing events rather than by mere verbal persuasion.

It is through such a revolving of attributes on both sides that the apparently hopeless deadlock of the Delphi scenes is ultimately resolved. This technique (or this intuition into life's actual workings?) seems to be traceable in the other plays of Aeschylus' second group also. We have seen indications of a turning of the Danaids' character in the opposite sense, from fair to foul, in *The Suppliants* trilogy; and it may appear from our consideration of the Prometheus plays that the apparent contradictions in *Prometheus Bound* can best be explained— perhaps can *only* be explained—by the assumption that the characters of Prometheus and Zeus were also turned as the trilogy progressed. *The Eumenides*, however, provides the most easily studied case history of the process, because here alone it can be followed in its entirety. During its first stage, in the Delphi scenes, the Furies are characterized by all parties, including themselves, as bestial creatures actuated purely by lust for the sinner's blood. The imagery of animals is applied to them repeatedly; they are likened to snakes (line 127), goats (196), lions (193), unnamed monsters which bloat themselves on human gore (183–84), and above all to bloodhounds (first at 131–32). That bestial aspect is all that we are permitted to see in them during the Delphi scenes; and as for Apollo, it is all that he ever manages to see in them. As late in the play as line 664, long after the animal imagery has been dropped by every other speaker, Apollo, being deftly outwitted by them in argument at the trial, resorts to shouting at them: "Beasts hateful every way!" So long as he alone represents the Olympians in their dealings with the Furies, there is not the slightest chance of an agreement. He remains throughout an inflexible doctrinaire.

Change can come only at Athens, and with the intervention of Athens's goddess. From Delphi to Athens the scene abruptly shifts at line 235, and we enter the long central movement of the play. It comprises, in brief, the arrival of Orestes at Athena's temple, followed at a short interval by that of the pursuing Furies; his appeal for the goddess's protection; her arrival from afar, and her persuasion of both parties to submit their quarrel to her discretion; and, finally, the trial and acquittal of Orestes before a jury of Athenians. Before we approach the climax of this movement, the trial—the most surreal of all scenes in extant Aeschylus—it will be rewarding to consider the nature of Athena and her effect on the Furies. Unlike the Delphic Apollo but like her namesake city of Athens, Athena proves able and willing to understand both parties in the dispute, the female and the male, the old and the new. Of all the deities of Olympus she is best fitted to mediate between these parties, because, in accordance with a tradition that in part is at least as old as Homer, she partakes of the attributes of both sexes. Already in Homer she is at once a virgin and a mighty force in battle. She is patroness of the traditionally feminine art of weaving, yet also, in post-Homeric times, of the traditionally masculine arts of the potter and the sculptor, who in archaic and classical Greece, especially in Athens, loved to represent her in a guise utterly paradoxical not only to an ancient Greek but also to the peoples of most cultures until well into the twentieth century: as a slender, delicate woman fully equipped as a heavy-armed infantryman.

In the opening scene at Athens, before the arrival of Athena, the Furies continue to display the bestial aspect that they had displayed at Delphi: "it smiles at me, the reek of human blood," they cry at their first arrival, as like hounds they cast around for their victim, Orestes (line 253; for other animal imagery applied by the Furies to themselves during this episode, compare 264–67, 302, 305, 326). After that arrival there are no more hints of animality in the play, with the exception of that put into the mouth of Apollo at line 664. Athena's courteous opening words to them immediately set a new tone. Responding to her with equal courtesy and moderation, they quietly explain their function in the cosmos, which is now represented as the seeking out and punishment for familial murders; and they, as well as Orestes, agree to entrust the decision in their case to Athena. When she has listened to both parties, she announces (lines 470–89) that in so difficult a case the only recourse is to a *trial*—a trial before a court of Athenian citizens.

At this point yet another of those verbal and moral ambiguities that have haunted the two earlier plays of the *Or-*

esteia begins to be resolved. So far in the trilogy we have heard many conflicting appeals by all parties to *dikē,* a word which up to now has been quite fairly translatable into English as "justice," in the contexts in which it has appeared. But "justice" is only one of a wide range of meanings that *dikē* may possess in Greek, and that—unfortunately for translators of the *Oresteia* and their readers—have to be rendered by a correspondingly wide range of different English words. Among those meanings, one that occurs with increasing frequency in the litigious democracy of fifth-century Athens is "trial." In the episode following this speech of Athena, a *dikē,* at last defined in this sense, will be enacted before the audience's eyes. Such an evolution from ambiguity toward definition, first in the word, finally in the visually manifested thing, will be familiar enough by this stage in our progress through the plays, but this instance seems outstandingly significant for the interpretation of the entire trilogy. Whatever the result of the forthcoming trial may turn out to be, we have at this point suddenly leapt forward from the era of the interminable human or even divine vendetta, in which each successive participant claims the sanction of his own *dikē* as "justice," to an era in which the body politic intervenes to decide once for all which claim may stand by means of *dikē* as "trial." And this leap from the primaeval past into the present (in some sense, not merely the present of Aeschylus and his contemporaries, but also our own) has been made possible by Athena and in her city, Athens.

Not surprisingly, it will be long before the Furies can accept this utterly unforeseen development. Even as Athena leaves to select a jury from the Athenian citizenry, they break into a song (lines 490–565) in which they appeal throughout to *dikē,* but in its most ancient sense: that of a goddess, Justice personified. Her rights and theirs, they sing, are threatened by this new institution, a trial at law. If the matricide Orestes goes free as a result of it, henceforth no one, whether father or mother, will any longer be able to call on Justice or the Furies for vengeance. "The house of Justice is collapsing!" (line 516), for no man will revere her if he is not held in check by fear of punishment. Then follows a very significant appeal, whether to the audience, to Athens, or to mankind is left unclear in the context (lines 526–30):

> Do not accept the life of anarchy,
> Nor yet the life of tyranny!
> For to the middle way,
> In all things, God has granted victory!

To state the drift of the song as a whole, there is a traditional morality (the Furies name it, or rather her, *Dikē*) that transcends the proceedings of any human law court, and society will fall apart if that morality is not enforced by an element of fear. On the other hand, the man who respects it may live prosperously and without constraints. Here is yet another gentle revolution in the character of the Furies. Contact with the intelligent and civilized patron goddess of Athens has brought out a side of them at which one could never have guessed while watching their earlier confrontation with the blustering Apollo. They remain determined to punish the matricide, but their motivation is no longer that of the bloodhound programmed solely to seek out and destroy. They justify their determination by a principle with which, so far as it goes, few thoughtful persons of any society in any era could disagree. Certainly Athena does not, as will be seen shortly.

After the end of that choral song, the imagined setting seems to change from Athena's temple and image on the Acropolis to the top of the low hill that lies just to the west of it, the Areopagus. This, of course, is the very place in which the Athenian court of Areopagus held its sessions in Aeschylus' day, as it had always done throughout the recorded history of the city. The dispute over the status of this court, as was seen above (p. 24), was the focal point of the fierce constitutional struggle of the years ca. 463–458 B.C., which ended in the triumph of the new democracy under the leadership of Pericles. Until that crisis, the court had not only held jurisdiction over many areas of legal dispute but had also exercised very wide and not very clearly defined powers over the government of Athens in general. To the democrats, bent on securing a system that would allow direct participation of all the citizens in the executive magistracies, the legislative assembly, and the law courts, such an archaic and unrepresentative institution was plainly intolerable. They succeeded eventually, amid great factional violence, in stripping the Areopagus court of all its prerogatives except jurisdiction in homicide cases and a few politically insignificant ritual functions. Thus, in this trial scene, the action of the *Oresteia* has moved from far away heroic Argos to focus on the heart and center of the contemporary political struggle in Athens: a hill, and a court, that were the major symbols of that struggle. The atmosphere in the Theater of Dionysus, as this point gradually became clear, may well have been charged with lightning: what would the poet say—what *could* he say—that was not certain to outrage the convictions of about half his audience? It may perhaps be at this point that one begins fully to realize the majesty and the danger of the project that Aeschylus had undertaken in the *Oresteia*: a diagnosis of the political and spiritual ills both of the very ancient way of life and of the very new; to be followed, in the last few minutes of the trilogy, by a magnificent symbolic enactment in spectacle and music of the only cure.

Aeschylean surrealism reaches its acme in the trial scene. That a jury of human beings should sit to vote on a case that has divided the powers of Heaven and Earth, the attorneys for the prosecution being daughters of Night and nieces of Fate, while the defense counsel is a son of Zeus and his spokesman! It is fantastic; and yet at a different level the scene hits the deep truth of the intellectual, political, and religious crisis that was upon the Athenian of 458 B.C. He was moving fast into a world wherein, literally, *the onus of judging rests on the human being*, even when he must judge between gods. The arguments presented to the court by counsel are, simply considered as instruments of rational persuasion, scarcely more plausible than the setting of the trial as a whole (how could they be?). It is no wonder that neither counsel in fact proves to have brought over the jury to his side, but that the eventual vote is split down the middle. On the other hand, their arguments do achieve what was surely the dramatist's intended effect: to bring out at their most vivid the natures of the contestants and of the issues involved in the struggle, whether on the divine level or on the contemporary political one.

With admirable evenhandedness, Aeschylus assigns far readier legal wits to the Furies than he does to their powerful opponents. They drive first Orestes (lines 604–13) and then even Apollo (640–56) into apparent logical impasses. Apollo only extracts himself by abruptly switching his attack to their fundamental premise (expressed concisely at lines 602–08): that the guilt of matricide outweighs the guilt of husband-murder because the former violates blood ties, the latter does not; to the Furies it is the female, not the male, who creates the child and thus guarantees the perpetuation of the clan. And it is with that primaeval and natural social unit, the clan, and its values, that they are concerned, not with any later and artificial unit such as a city. Apollo's counterblast to that premise may well have knocked many of the audience flat, and has continued to dumbfound many of Aeschylus' critics down to the present day (lines 658–61): "She who is called the mother of a child is not its creator, but only the nurse of the newly sown seed. The creator is he who begets; *she* keeps safe the plant for him, as a stranger for a stranger, granted God brings it to no harm." As a material witness to the accuracy of this statement, Apollo calls in very flattering language on Athena herself, who was born of no female but sprang perfect from the head of Zeus. He concludes the presentation of his case with a promise to ensure the future greatness of Athens, in part through Orestes who, if acquitted, will join his city of Argos in eternal alliance with Athena's city.

This, at first hearing, very surprising speech only begins to make sense in the dramatic and political context as one comes to realize that Apollo is here speaking with the voice of the liberal reformists of contemporary Athens. His promise of a permanent Argive alliance (which Orestes repeats and amplifies in his postacquittal speech, lines 762–74) can scarcely be anything but a direct reference to the total reversal of Athenian foreign policy that the Periclean party brought about concurrently with their central domestic enterprise, the reform of the Areopagus. Under the unreformed Areopagite regime that foreign policy had been firmly anchored on an alliance with Sparta, the most conservative, politically and intellectually, of the Greek city-states. The democrats abruptly broke off the Spartan alliance and allied Athens with Sparta's traditionally bitter enemy, Argos, which at that time seems also to have been governed under a form of democracy. Apollo's argument against the participation of the female in the process of conception seems equally to allude to a heated contemporary controversy, but in this case a scientific one. A number of Greek philosopher-scientists are known to have been debating this question during the middle decades of the fifth century, among them Pericles' friend Anaxagoras (see above, pp. 24–28). The evidence for the position that Anaxagoras took on it is somewhat confused, but our most reliable witness, Aristotle, implies that he argued, as Apollo does here, that the male's semen was the sole source of human life and that the womb merely constituted a receptacle for its growth. Thus the champion of the male defendant in the trial scene of *The Eumenides* is now seen to favor views which the audience could scarcely have failed to identify, respectively, with those of the newly triumphant democratic reformers and of the advanced thinkers in the circle of Pericles.

After that speech both parties rest their cases. Before the crucial vote is taken, however, Athena intervenes in the proceedings with a long speech (lines 681–710) in which she proclaims that this court, summoned ad hoc for the trial of Orestes, is to exist henceforth forever in her city as the court of Areopagus. Day and night alike, she foretells, this court will keep watch over Athens, and the fear of it will restrain the citizens from unjust action. In this context she adds some general advice on political conduct (lines 696–99)

> I urge my citizens to revere and keep
> That state which is not anarchy or tyranny,
> And not to expel all terror from the city.
> What human being is just when freed from fear?

Notable in these lines is the community of feeling between Athena and the Furies, who have voiced the same opinions in very nearly the same words at lines 517–30. The speech as a whole, indeed, seems designed to conciliate those conservative Athenians—the human counterparts of the Furies—to

whom the Areopagus had always been the most important
and most stable element in the governing of the city. In this
Athena's diplomacy is exquisite. Her praise of the Areopagus
is unbounded, yet the only function of the court she mentions
specifically is that for which she has summoned it on the
present occasion: a homicide trial. And this, as we saw, was
the one signficant function the reforming democrats had left
to it anyway.

While the silent Areopagite jurors cast their voting-peb-
bles into the ballot urns (lines 711 and following), Apollo and
the Furies exchange pointed insults. As the voting draws to
a close, Athena announces that she too will cast her pebble—
in favor of Orestes, since she belongs to the male side, the
side of her sole parent, Zeus; even should the human votes
be equal, therefore, Orestes will win his case. The count of
votes begins, while the anxious litigants exclaim, in the con-
trasting imagery that has pervaded the *Oresteia* from its beginning (744–46):

> *Orestes:* Shining Apollo, how will the trial be judged?
> *Chorus:* Black mother Night, do you behold this thing?
> *Orestes:* Now shall I die by the noose—or see the light!

The votes prove, in fact, to be even; the human beings have
been no less in favor of the female/dark than of the male/light.
Orestes escapes punishment for his matricide by a hair's
breadth, through that gentle pressure laid on the scales by
the patron deity of Athens, who is something between the
male and the female, who, like her citizens in 458 B.C., has
her being in the "no-man's-land of dark and light." (That
enigmatic Aeschylean phrase, which seemed the appropriate
epigraph for this final chapter, comes from the opening
chorus of *The Libation-Bearers*, line 63).

And so Orestes goes free, having found that deliverance

from his pains which Apollo had promised him at the beginning of the play, and having beheld at last a light that does
not delude. The human family feud is done with. Apollo, too,
has left the scene by now, although at what point we do not
know. In our text of the play his last speech is at lines 748–
51, where he bids the jurors count the votes. The *Oresteia* as
a whole represents Apollo as an unsympathetic being, from
Agamemnon 1202–12, where Cassandra relates how he punished her for refusing to make love to her ("What?" says the
Chorus there, "A *God* struck by desire?"), through the description of his fantastic threats to Orestes should he fail to
carry out the matricide in *The Libation-Bearers* 269–96, to his
onstage behavior in *The Eumenides*. He is an extremist in all
his relationships with the feminine principle; it is surely significant that the last mythological exploit of his of which we
hear in *The Eumenides* (lines 723–28) is the bizarre tale of how
he cheated those most august of pre-Olympian goddesses, the
Fates, by making them drunk. But neither the finale of the
Oresteia nor the Athens of 458 B.C., of which it is an ideal
projection, have any place for extremists. Apollo leaves without farewells.

As we enter the third and last movement of *The Eumenides*
(lines 778–1047) there remain in the *orchēstra* the threatening
black rectangle formed by the Chorus, and Athena, perhaps
in front of the *skēnē* and facing them; behind her we may well
imagine the still silent jurors of the Areopagus, representing
the people of her city. It at once appears that the acquittal of
Orestes, however happy for him, has raised terrible problems,
in its turn, for the city and the cosmos. The Furies break into
a frantic song and dance of hate against the "younger Gods,"
the Olympians, and against the land and people of Athens.
Here we must revert for the last time in this account of *The
Eumenides* to the phenomenon that I have called the "turning"

of the Furies' character. We have seen how they appeared in
the early scenes of the play as utterly revolting creatures,
characterized primarily as animals in form and instinct. So
they remained as long as they were confronted only by the
divine and human males Apollo and Orestes. With the epiphany of the androgynous Athena, their animal characteristics
have faded out and they have taken on the aspect of highly
articulate conservatives, upholding the perpetuation of immemorially ancient traditions in both cosmic and human affairs, with a ready and sometimes even entertaining wit. And
so they have remained, on the whole, until the acquittal of
Orestes. Nevertheless, as early as their first encounter with
Athena there has been a hint of yet another aspect of their
nature. Even as she decides to prepare for a trial, Athena is
apprehensive of this aspect (lines 477–79): supposing their
case is defeated, "hereafter poison shall proceed out of their
angry spirits, poison falling on the land as an unbearable,
unending plague." As the crisis of the trial approaches, the
Furies do in fact utter threats against the Attic landscape
(lines 711 and 720), and Apollo taunts them in these words
(729–30): "In a moment you are going to lose this case and
vomit up that poison of yours, but it won't do your enemies
the slightest harm!"

This new aspect that the Furies are gradually turning
toward the audience is, like the former ones, perfectly con-
gruous with their fundamental character as female earth-
dwellers. As we saw early in this book, Earth not merely hides
within her the dead and the places of judgment, but she is
also responsible for the fertility of the humans, animals, and
plants that exist on her surface. The Furies are now emerging
as fertility goddesses, with the power to blight or prosper the
life of nature at their will. In the raging song with which they
open the third movement of the play, they threaten to turn

the destructive side of this power against Athens, in horrific
words that might equally apply to the effects of nuclear ra-
diation (lines 782–86):

> Shooting from my very heart
> Poison, poison for my pain;
> It shall drip upon your land
> Unbearable, and from it rise
> Canker blasting leaf and child
>   (HEAR ME, JUSTICE!)
> Canker racing through the plain!

In the ensuing interchange, lasting until line 919, Athena
takes hold of this fertility function of the Furies and works to
convert it from its destructive to its creative aspect. As she
talks to them, their wild outbursts of song and dance grow
shorter, until at line 892 they are calm enough at last to engage
with her in spoken line-for-line dialogue. Athena meets their
rage with gentle persuasion, with promises of an honored
place in the human and divine community of Athens, and, at
one point (lines 826–29), with a delicate reminder that she has
direct access to Zeus's thunderbolt arsenal. (In this situation,
too, the principle that she shares with the Furies holds good,
as it continues to hold good in most compacts, whether between individuals or between nations: there must be an element of fear, but it must not be the sole element.) Toward the
end of the line-by-line dialogue they tentatively begin to yield
to Athena's offer of an honored home in a city whose future
promises ever more honor. What hymn, they ask her, would
she have them sing over her land? Athena's answer to that
begins with language (lines 903–09) that might remind one
of Aphrodite's language in her speech on the marriage of
Earth and Sky, in *The Danaides*:

> Blessings to suit a blameless victory!
> Blessings from the earth and from the ocean waters
> And from the sky! Pray that the airy winds
> Breathe sunshine as they march across the land,
> That the yields of earth and cattle never fail
> My citizens, but thrive to overflowing,
> That human seed in safety ever grow!

She concludes by asking the Furies also to foster piety and justice in her city (in this, appealing to the different aspect of themselves which they have revealed in the middle movement of the play) and by predicting a glorious future for Athens in external wars.

As Athena ends this speech, the Furies break into a joyous song and dance, each stanza of which is answered in an equally joyous recitative passage by Athena. In the course of this marvelous antiphony the Furies happily accept residency (*metoikia*) in Athens, calling down on the city all the blessings that Athena has asked for, and more besides. They appeal to the Fates, as "spirits of right law" (line 963), to grant health and happy marriage to the Athenian youth. They pray that "the thunder of Strife, who cannot eat her fill of evils, may never be heard in this city" (976–78), and that there be no "dooms of murder answering murder" (982), but that the citizens "may exchange joys for joys among each other in a spirit of mutual love, and may hate the enemy as with one mind, for this is the way to cure many of the evils among humanity" (984–87). Toward the end of the singing a procession of citizens is forming under Athena's orders, and after the last exultant stanza dies away she proclaims that this procession is to escort the Furies with the glare of torchlight to their new home, a cave beneath the earth (presumably identifiable with the shrine at the foot of the Areopagus hill, which was shown

as theirs to visitors in later antiquity). This speech of Athena's
(lines 1021–31), as we now have it in the few manuscripts of
The Eumenides, has almost certainly been mutilated in trans-
mission. Two ancient accounts of the play mention that "after
Athena had calmed the Furies" she gave them a new name,
Eumenides—that is, the Kindly Ones. No such passage occurs in the text of *The Eumenides* which has survived in the
manuscripts, but the very title of the play proves that it must
once have existed, and the obvious place for it would be here.
Such a formal reversal in the Chorus's name would not merely
be a fitting culmination to the reversal in its feelings wrought
by Athena; it would also fit very well with the two magnificent visual gestures that either accompanied this speech or
took place immediately after it. At lines 1025–26 Athena orders:

> By draping them in cloaks of crimson dye
> Honor them, and let the light of fire move on!

Thus, in these final moments of the trilogy, the black rectangle
that has dominated the dancing floor since the mourning
chorus entered at the beginning of *The Libation-Bearers* turns
to crimson, as attendants throw the cloaks round the shoul-
ders of the Kindly Ones. The symbolism of this gesture may
be more complex than appears at first sight. It is known that
at Athens' greatest civic festival, the Panathenaea, the resi-
dent aliens (*metoikoi*) marched in the procession wearing crimson robes; thus the new dress visually clinches the Kindly
Ones' acceptance of their new status of *metoikia* in the city.
But this is also the third occasion in the trilogy on which the
theater has been brightened by wide expanses of colored dra-
pery. The former two were the Tapestry Scene of *Agamemnon,*
in which the king walked on purple to his death, and the
scene in *The Libation-Bearers* where Orestes, standing over the

dead bodies of his mother and Aegisthus, had the attendants hold up the bloody murder-robe. Like so many other images in the *Oresteia*, verbal and visual, the colored cloth that had been a symbol of dread becomes, at the end, a symbol of joy and reconciliation.

The final visual gesture is the great flaring of torches as the procession, headed by Athena (see lines 1003–05), moves off to lead the Kindly Ones, "children of Night no more her children" (line 1034) toward their new home under the earth. Here an image that has recurred ambiguously in words throughout the trilogy, from the prologue of *Agamemnon* onward, is finally made visible and given a definitive and joyful meaning. The retreat of the light back toward the darkness of the cave of the Kindly Ones signifies the end of the feud between male and female (in both their literal and figurative senses) in the family, the city, and the cosmos. As the escorting citizens sing in the very last words of *The Eumenides*, the two ultimate principals in that feud, the Father of the Olympians and the pre-Olympian Goddess of Destiny, are now at one:

> Thus Zeus the all seeing
> And Fate have come together;
>   Cry out for joy at this our song!

The torchlights, the crimson robes, disappear through the side entrance; the tragedy (or comedy, or masque, or dream?) is ended. The *Oresteia* production, however, is not. After this the audience sits back and smiles over the satyr-play *Proteus* (see fragment S 119, with Smyth's comments), which tells of Agamemnon's brother Menelaus, marooned among the merry satyrs on an islet near the Egyptian coast, to which he has strayed during his voyage home from the pitiless sack of Troy—so long ago, it now seems.

Prometheus Bound

The profundities of the *Oresteia* trilogy, like those of a dream, cannot be fully indicated, let alone definitively interpreted, in a few pages of prose, or even in a thousand. In the end, a lyrical drama of this scale and splendor must be confronted by each reader and sensed out in all its lyric and dramatic dimensions. All I hope to have achieved in the preceding sketch is to alert readers to certain techniques, certain major lines of dramatic development, and certain historical circumstances, the understanding of which may help them along the way toward such a confrontation. The profundities of the *Prometheus Bound* seem equal to those of the *Oresteia*, while any interpretation is far more hazardous because here we are dealing with only a fragment of a once vast design. Yet one broad generalization seems to me to apply quite certainly to both works: they can have proceeded only from a mind that at some point had looked on chaos—chaos intellectual, political, and religious.

The proud and unyielding rebel against higher authority must be among the oldest and most widespread figures in world storytelling, as in the actual life of all peoples. Extant Greek literature opens with this very theme. It is worth recalling, in our present context, the story-pattern of the *Iliad*. The chieftain Achilles, conscious of his personal superiority to his overlord, Agamemnon, in lineage (for Achilles' mother is divine) and in military prowess, quarrels with him and refuses to fight. For long after their great quarrel in *Iliad* I their enmity seems irreconcilable, as the Embassy in *Iliad* IX emphasizes above all. Yet after terrible private and communal sufferings on all sides the two are in fact reconciled, when Agamemnon in *Iliad* XIX publicly acknowledges Achilles' greatness and makes what material amends he can to his affronted honor. When last we see the pair of them together, in *Iliad* XXIII, they are happily watching the athletic sports, and the final episode of that book shows the knightly Achilles making a reciprocal gesture of profound respect to Agamemnon's kingliness. We shall see some reasons for supposing that the *Prometheia* (in this chapter I shall adopt that term for Aeschylus' group of tragedies on the Prometheus theme; see the Table of Dates) as it originally stood may have displayed a similar overall story-pattern.

Its opening situation, a quarrel between the rebel conscious of his own high lineage (for the Aeschylean Prometheus is son of the primal divinity, Earth) and prowess, and the authoritarian monarch, seems quite close to the opening situation of the *Iliad*. The significant differences reside first in the nature of Prometheus' prowess, and second in the towering divine status of each contestant: this quarrel is between the supreme God of the Olympians, on the one hand, and a Titan (that is, a member of the divine generation that ruled in heaven before the Olympians), on the other. These differences must be considered in turn if we are to put this most influential and most puzzling of Aeschylus' plays into its historical perspective. First, the prowess on which Prometheus prides himself is the very antitype of Achilles' military valor: it is the prowess of the mind. In earlier Greek story, from Hesiod's epics down to Aeschylus' own work of 472 B.C., the satyr-play *Prometheus Pyrkaeus*, the central motif of the Prometheus legend had been a simple and primitive one which can be paralleled in many early cultures right across the globe: Prometheus had stolen fire from the gods by trickery and had bestowed this great gift on mortals. In *Prometheus Bound*, that theft is still the first charge laid against him by Zeus and the other gods, but it is only one of several, and its implications far transcend the mere theft of an element. In this play it is

only an essential first step in a grandiose program of bene-
faction toward humanity. For fire is *pantechnon*, "means of all
arts" (this is already declared at line 7), and Prometheus' gift
of it proves to be a powerful symbol for a vast array of intellectual as well as technological inventions that he has conferred on mortals. The Titan catalogues these majestically in
the pair of speeches at lines 436–71 and 476–506, which modern students often refer to as the "Culture Speeches." Mankind, says Prometheus, lived in a dreary confusion, "like so
many dream-phantoms" (lines 448–49), until he revealed to
them the arts of architecture, astronomy, mathematics ("pre-
eminent among the works of the intelligence," 459), alpha-
betic writing, the domestication of animals, ship-building, the
reading of the future in dreams and other omens, and me-
tallurgy. He concludes the astonishing list thus (lines 505–06):

> In one short word hear all:
> All arts come from Prometheus to mankind!

All this, he claims elsewhere in the play (notably in lines 199–
243), was carried out in flat defiance of Zeus. So far had
Zeus's purpose been from advancing primitive mankind in
any intellectual or material respect, that he had actually
planned to wipe out our miserable species altogether. It is for
having frustrated this plan, no less than for the transference
of fire from heaven to earth, that Prometheus is now being
punished by that cruel and arbitrary tyrant.

The conflict that Aeschylus thus sets up in this play between Prometheus and Zeus is a conflict of intellectual and
political principles such as neither Homer nor Hesiod, living
when and where they did, could ever have dreamed of; for
such a conflict could scarcely have been observable in any
society earlier than the Athens (and perhaps also the Sicily)
of Aeschylus' later years. It may seem that in the *Prometheia*,

just as in the *Oresteia*, the poet is identifying and exploring a phenomenon which was emerging in his city for almost the first time in history, but which has been endemic in Western civilization ever since. This time he lays his finger on the conflict between the innovative intellectual, whether philosopher, scientist, or technologist, and the political authority determined to preserve its rule unchanged, free from question or comment. Hereafter it will be witnessed again and again throughout history: the trial and condemnation of Socrates within two generations after Aeschylus, the conflict between the Stoic philosophers and the early Roman emperors, the relationship between revolutionary and tsar, are only a few of the obvious examples. Perceiving this phenomenon at its first appearance, Aeschylus dramatized it, as always, in the only language that was as yet freely and universally understood by his fellow citizens, the language of myth. And in this case he reached back for the appropriate story to a mythic period not too long after the very beginnings of the universe.

This brings us to the second major qualitative difference between the basic situations of the *Iliad* and the *Prometheia*: in the latter the rebel and the ruler are both great deities. Prometheus, in fact, is as ancient and venerable a deity as Zeus, so far as genealogy is concerned; but it is the involvement of Zeus in the conflict, and the characterization that he receives in *Prometheus Bound*, that have most perplexed the critics. Many have found it hard or impossible to reconcile this characterization, as they perceive it, with the supposedly reverential treatment that Zeus receives elsewhere in Aeschylus; and to some able scholars during the past century or so it has even formed one ground for a denial of Aeschylus' authorship of our play. To me, the furor seems to result at least in part from an excusable misapprehension about the nature of ancient Greek religion, combined with, perhaps, an insufficient appreciation of an important feature of late-Aeschylean dramaturgy, combined with a deplorable historical accident—the fact that Time has deprived us of all but the first play of the *Prometheia*. This last fact above all needs to be kept more firmly in mind than it customarily is throughout any debate on the significance of *Prometheus Bound*. From first to last, Aeschylus is a master of paradox and reversal. His dramas are such that in none of them could the unwary spectator safely predict the denouement from the opening episodes; only with long experience of our poet, and after close inspection, may one detect the more or less subliminal clues—usually verbal—that have been included in the beginning as pointers to the end. For instance, how much should we certainly know of the overall developments of the *Oresteia* if only *Agamemnon*, or even *Agamemnon* and *The Libation-Bearers* together, had been left to us? Or even of a single play, *The Seven Against Thebes*, if our manuscripts had broken off at line 652? We should never allow ourselves to be misled by the evident artistic completeness of the *Prometheus Bound* into forgetting that thematically this play (just like *The Suppliants*) is a fragment, rudely torn from its original context by the chances of preservation. It is only the first movement of a most carefully designed verbal and visual symphony, the rest of which is almost entirely beyond our hearing.

This is one problem to be kept in mind as we turn to the apparent characterization of Zeus in *Prometheus Bound*, but here we face a further and unique difficulty. From the later centuries of classical antiquity until within living memory, the vast majority of Aeschylus' commentators were professed Christians, and many of them, indeed, Christian clergy. Even at the present day most of his commentators and readers are probably, if not committed to a particular faith, at any rate

brought up in a society in which the only model for religion
has for centuries been the Jewish or Christian model. Almost
by instinct we associate the idea of religion with a sacrosanct
book or books, a fixed body of doctrine, and above all a timeless and unchanging Supreme Being characterized from the
era of the Patriarchs until very recently as the Father, whose
nature has been revealed in the scriptures and interpreted for
believers by scholars of the church. It requires a conscious
effort to assimilate the facts that the religion of Aeschylus and
his fellow Greeks was polytheistic, that it rested on no sacred
book but on a bewildering multitude of traditional beliefs and
local cult-practices, that it possessed no universal priestly hierarchy, and that (as Edward Gibbon generalized with complete accuracy) "the devotion of the Pagans was not
incompatible with the most licentious scepticism." I have
often thought that only a Hindu, sharing as he ultimately does
in the same religious tradition as that from which the classical
Greek religion derived, could write a perfectly satisfactory
commentary on Aeschylus from this point of view. How much
could the learned and venerable Professor Godbole of *A Passage to India*, whose "conversations frequently culminated in
a cow," enlarge our understanding of the Io legend! Even,
however, when a citizen of the West has readjusted his imagination to the greatest extent possible, he is still apt to be
influenced by his society's long memory of the Judaeo-Chris-
tian God when he comes to contemplate the supreme deity
of the Greek pantheon, the Homeric "Father of Gods and
men." Hence arise the expectations implicit in many discus-
sions of the Aeschylean Zeus (but not of the Hera described
in *The Suppliants*, for instance, or of the Apollo manifest in
the *Oresteia*) that all Aeschylus' references to him ought somehow to be compatible with a vision of an unchanging, transcendent, wise, and even—for some commentators—a loving

deity. When, inevitably, a scholar comes upon a passage or a play that apparently does not fit this pattern, the way is wide open for attacks on the poet's consistency or even the authenticity of the texts concerned.

The realities of Aeschylus' mind and art seem to have been far different. He was not, and in the climate of pagan Greek religion could have not dreamed of being, a systematic expositor of a fixed theology. He was a sharp-eyed and sensitive observer of a city in which all things, not excluding perceptions of the traditional gods, were changing at a bewildering pace. He was, further, a poet-dramatist performing at the heart of that volatile city, sensing and amplifying its bewilderment at that clash between the old opinions and the new. Consequently, in his later plays, he represented opinions on either side with all the poetic force at his command. In the finale of the *Oresteia* he certainly reached a synthesis between the opposed opinions, and Aphrodite's speech in *The Danaides* may suggest that he ended *The Suppliants* trilogy in a somewhat similar way. Even granted that, however, the fact remains that we are still dealing with *dramas*—with attempts in the theater to explore the way life is or should be, through the medium of myth or image. The finale of a drama, even of an *Oresteia*, cannot be received as having the philosophic or dogmatic force of the conclusion to a Thoman syllogism. Rather than lay down the theological law about the nature of Zeus, Aeschylus seems to illuminate and try to harmonize a vast range of opinions about it. Some members of the Athenian audience during his last years may have envisioned Zeus as a rampant bull, some as an omnipotent deity who could execute his will by the mere power of thought, some (Anaxagoras, for instance?) as an obsolete despot who deserved to be toppled from his throne by a humanity that had at last progressed into philosophical enlightenment, some as the all

too human father of the Olympian family familiar to them
from Homer's epics (epics which were publicly recited to great
crowds at the Panathenaea festival throughout Aeschylus'
lifetime and long afterward). Each of these opinions is represented by one character or another, at one point or another,
in the later plays of Aeschylus.

This is one consideration that should perhaps give us
pause before we condemn *Prometheus Bound* as inconsistent
with Aeschylus' other work in its approach to Zeus. An
equally important consideration is the dramaturgical technique of Aeschylus which I call "turning," of which the most
notable example has been seen in *The Eumenides*. Earlier in
this section I raised the question how, or whether, we should
be able accurately to interpret the drift of the *Oresteia* or of
The Seven Against Thebes if the latter parts of those dramas had
happened not to be preserved. Here a similar question may
be asked with regard to *The Eumenides*. Suppose that the play's
text had been preserved only as far as the end of the movement set in Delphi, should we not in all reason conclude from
the descriptions of the Furies, from their actions, and from
the imagery applied to them, that Aeschylus considered them
and would persuade his audience to consider them as black
and hellish hags, good for nothing but to suck the blood of
any matricide who happened to be available? As it is, thanks
to the persistence of a handful of Byzantine copyists, we possess the entire text of the play and are able to analyze the
stages by which Aeschylus unobtrusively converts them into
crimson-clad guardians of fertility and law and order. Now
Prometheus Bound appears, like the Delphi episodes of *The Eumenides*, to represent only the first movement of the drama in
which it stood. The general analogy alone might suggest that
a character painted, on the whole, in such dark colors as Zeus
is painted by his adversary in *Prometheus Bound* might well

have taken on a different character in the later part of the trilogy. But there are also certain features in *Prometheus Bound* itself, and in the fragments of *Prometheus Unbound*, which reinforce that suggestion; it appears that the turning technique was applied here, too. Before we examine the evidence for this, however, let us review the course and dramatic characteristics of *Prometheus Bound* as it stands.

The mythic story that Aeschylus chose for this dramatization of the emerging opposition between skill and power entailed a theatrical experiment which cannot be matched for boldness in any other Attic tragedy. He was setting himself the task of making credible onstage an action that was set almost as far back in time and as far out in space as the ancient Greek imagination could reach. It was an action in which almost all the participants were necessarily divine or even elemental powers. Perhaps most formidable of all, from a dramatist's point of view, was the circumstance that the protagonist had necessarily to be immobile from near the beginning of the play until its very end—not merely unable to exit at any time during its course, but unable even to gesture. Correspondingly, the dramaturgy of *Prometheus Bound* is paralleled in no other Attic tragedy, and indeed in no play of any period that I am acquainted with. There is significant onstage action only at the beginning and end: in the prologue, where the Titan is dragged in by the emissaries of Zeus, Power and Violence (even what we should call abstract entities have roles in the *Prometheia*), and cruelly pinned to the sides of the lofty mountain chasm which is the imagined setting of the play; and in the exodus, where he disappears into the chasm amid a wild storm of all the elements.

There is no reliable evidence as to how these scenes were staged in the original production, nor as to how the entrances of the Chorus of Ocean's daughters (for which see lines 123–

35), or of Ocean himself (286–89, compare 397–99), or of Hermes (941) were managed. Some have assumed the need for a highly elaborate stage setting, complete with machinery, to swing at least some of these characters on and off the scene. But it might be argued that all one really needs for a performance of this play is a plank to which Prometheus may be bound, or perhaps not even the plank; everything could be (and in some modern productions actually has been) made clear by the poetry, reinforced here and there by dance and mime. In any view, however, a great part of the plot is carried by *words*, words that transport the spectator far from the dramatic location and time: to the far past and future, and to the utmost, monster-ridden regions of that mythological world-map which was outlined in chapter 4. In this, *Prometheus Bound* recalls *Agamemnon*, also the first play in its trilogy and also largely devoted to a research, through words, into distant times and places. But there is a notable difference. In *Prometheus Bound* the words are necessarily exchanged between the stationary hero and a succession of visitors each of whom appears one by one and, with the exception of the Chorus, departs to make room for another. All is focused on Prometheus; even the Chorus never addresses a word to any character but him until the last moments of the play, when it is given a brief exchange with Hermes (lines 1054–79). Between prologue and exodus, Prometheus is not merely the central figure of the play. He *is* the play, so far as its dramatic development is concerned, for this development consists in the progressive revelation of his nature and past history, his knowledge of the future, and his mounting rage against Zeus. Again, neither classical nor postclassical drama seems to offer any parallel to this motionless hero within whom all the essential dramatic action resides.

The main body of the play consists of two great expository movements. In the first of them, from Prometheus' first utterance at line 88 to the entrance of Io following line 560, we are introduced to the nature and status of Prometheus, to the violent upheaval in the politics of the early universe at the transition from the rule of Kronos to that of Zeus, and to Prometheus' benefactions to humanity. Aeschylus' apparently quite unprecedented version of all these matters in itself entailed exposition of them on a grand scale. Over everything that happens broods a terrible figure, Zeus. He is represented at all points as a savage, faithless, and ungrateful tyrant over gods and humanity. The Greek words *tyrannos* and *tyrannis*, "tyrant" and "tyranny," are repeatedly applied to him and his rule, and not in their neutral archaic sense, in which they denoted simply monarchic power: Zeus is given many of the characteristics that Herodotus and Plato assign to "tyranny" in the evil political and moral sense which it has retained ever since in the languages of the West. More than once, however, speakers emphasize that his tyranny is *new* (lines 35, 148–51, 310), since Zeus has only recently overthrown his father, Kronos, in the great struggle between the Titans and the Olympians, as described in lines 199–221. That emphasis on newness may be significant, especially in the light of Prometheus' cry later in the play (line 982):

But Time, as Time grows older, teaches all.

Whereas that first expository movement centers on the political aspect of Zeus's tyranny over the universe, and in particular on his cruel treatment of his opponent Prometheus, the second movement (lines 561–886) develops in terrible detail, visual as well as verbal, the tyrant's wanton lust and savagery toward a defenseless human being. With the wild entrance of the cow-horned Io, Aeschylus at last presents to our eyes that strange figure which had loomed unseen through so much of the singing and dialogue of *The Suppliants*. The Danaid chorus in that play had dwelt above all on the triumphant ending of Io's wanderings across the face of the earth. *Prometheus Bound*, on the contrary, presents her to us at the time when she is still in the midst of that torment brought upon her by Zeus's passion; when she has been reduced to a half-animal state in body and mind. Both movements, then, conspire to present a Zeus who, at the dramatic time of this play, exemplifies the faults that the Greeks traditionally attributed to the tyrant at his worst. Yet there are also several indications in both that at some later time he will reveal a different face, and that Prometheus, too, is not as absolute in his enmity toward Zeus as one might have gathered from a superficial reading or hearing. These signs that Aeschylus may eventually have broken the deadlock between the two by means of the turning technique are worth a close look.

There are contradictions in Prometheus' statements and violent shifts in his emotions that may remind one partly of the Danaids, partly of (for example) the Watchman and the Chorus of *Agamemnon*; again in this play we seem to be living in that nightmare world in which nothing is fixed, nothing is quite what it seems to be. The contradictions appear immediately in Prometheus' magnificent opening utterance, which is partly spoken, partly chanted, and partly sung (this alternation between the three modes of delivery within a single utterance, unique in Greek tragedy, is probably meant to emphasize rhythmically the inconsistencies that we are discussing). He laments that he can see no way out of his sufferings (lines 98–100), then proclaims that he knows every detail of the future and that no pain can catch him unprepared (101–04); and yet again, as he hears the sounds made by the approaching Chorus, he cries out that he is "fearful of all that approaches me" (126). Helpless self-pity, majestic confidence, and terror all surface within that single speech. Even more surprising are the flat contradictions in Prometheus' prophecies. Through most of the play he progressively reveals his knowledge of a secret which, unless he declares it, will topple Zeus from his tyranny of the universe. His first hint of this comes at lines 168–79 and 189–92; there is a further allusion at 519–25; at 755–68 he expounds it in some detail to his human fellow sufferer, Io. The secret is that Zeus will err sexually once more, but that this time he will suffer deeply for his error, for he will marry a wife who is fated to bear a child greater than its father. By keeping the name of this woman to himself, Prometheus hopes that he will be able to force Zeus into releasing him. (Only from other ancient writers do we learn who the woman was; it was Thetis, who was married eventually to Peleus and bore him the greatest of all heroes in Greek legend, Achilles.) After Io has scampered offstage in a fresh paroxysm of madness caused by the gadfly's sting (lines 877–86), Prometheus is so carried away by indignation at what he has seen that he boldly shouts his knowledge of the fatal secret to the heavens (907–27). This leads immediately to the final scene of the play. Hermes, the messenger of Zeus, hurries down to demand the secret, threatening Prometheus with engulfment in the rock, to be followed, long after, by his reemergence into the light and his exposure to the daily attacks of an eagle which will gnaw at his liver. Even so, Prometheus scornfully refuses to deliver up his knowledge, and in a storm of all the elements he disappears into the chasm. With that tempestuous finale all hope for Prometheus and for humanity seems lost. The opposition between him and Zeus, between brute force and the powers of the mind, seems as irreconcilable as the opposition between Apollo and the Furies that was manifest in the last tableau of the Delphi movement in *The Eumenides*. Both scenes are images of a universe torn in two.

Against this picture of a crescendo of defiance and divine violence in the dramatic present of *Prometheus Bound* must be set certain Promethean visions of a far future in which Zeus will wear an utterly different aspect, in which he will continue to hold the lordship of the universe but will exercise it gently both toward the Titan Prometheus, who will be freely reconciled to him, and toward the human Io. A time will come, says Prometheus at the end of the opening sung and chanted dialogue between him and the Chorus (lines 188–92), when "Zeus's thought shall be softened, when he receives this hammer-blow [that is, when he realizes the threat posed to him by the secret of the fatal marriage that will depose him]. He shall calm that ineluctable rage, and in the end shall come to harmony and friendship with me, eagerly; and eagerly shall I also come." An agreement between Zeus and Prometheus that will be enthusiastically welcomed by both parties may well seem a bizarre fancy in the immediate context in which Prometheus mentions it. Even stranger, again if taken in its immediate dramatic context, is the vision he sees in the course of his final speech to Io (lines 823–76), a vision of deliverance for her and for himself. In that speech he first describes certain incidents in Io's earlier wanderings. They include her visit to the most famous of Zeus's oracles, that at Dodona, where the miraculous oak trees gave voice and expressly hailed her as "you who shall be the glorious wife of Zeus" (lines 834–35). Prometheus explains the meaning of that unexpected salutation in the second half of the speech, in a prophecy which he emphasizes is not his own but which he has heard from his mother, Themis—an august authority, for that name means "Rightness," and in this play, as we learn from lines 209–10, it is one of the many names for Earth herself. Io's wanderings, he says, will end at Kanobos on the Nile: "Here at last Zeus makes you sane, stroking (*epaphōn*) you with a hand that brings no terror, for he shall touch you only; and you shall bear dark Epaphus, who shall take his name from that begetting by Zeus" (lines 848–51). From Epaphus shall descend a glorious line, including the Danaids (lines 856–69, quoted above, pp. 96–97) and culminating in the great hero-god Herakles. And it is Herakles, says Prometheus, still on the authority of Themis-Earth, "who shall release me from these pains."

The moment that vision ends we are abruptly pulled back into the brutal dramatic present of *Prometheus Bound*. Stung by the gadfly, Io rushes away, screaming, into the next cruel stage of her wanderings—how cruel, we have heard from Prometheus' prophecies at lines 707–41 and 790–815, with their vistas of scorching deserts, thunderous rivers, and mountains whose peaks border on the stars, regions of the far east and south peopled by hostile and monstrous beings. (These speeches, of all Aeschylean speeches, need to be declaimed aloud in some echoing building. The poetry here, with its resonances of boundless space and its ringing, exotic names of places and peoples far remote, can be matched in our language only by the poetry of Milton, who in fact knew *Prometheus Bound* well.) But for a few moments, during that dislocation of time in Prometheus' final prophecy to Io, we have glimpsed far off in the future, a Zeus whose "hand brings no terror," an Io restored to herself, a nonviolent union between the divine male and the human female—and a Prometheus delivered. The very last phrase of the prophecy guaranteed by Themis-Earth, "who shall release me from these pains," is of special interest for another reason also. It and phrases of similar meaning, while found nowhere in the first group of Aeschylus' extant plays, recur in all those of the second group almost with the effect of a signature-tune. We have followed it from the exit song of *The Suppliants* (lines 1062–67, "Zeus . . . who completely *released Io from her sorrow,* checking with a healing hand, making violence into grace"), through the "deliverance from these pains" of the Watchman's speech (*Agamemnon*, lines 1 and 20; see above, pp. 117–18), and Apollo's promise to Orestes "utterly to deliver you from these pains" (*Eumenides* 83), into our present play, where indeed it recurs so often that it must be counted as a positive leitmotiv. It is found here at lines 262, 316, 326, 471, 749–50, 754, 773, and, as we have just seen, 872–73, on some occasions with reference to Prometheus and on others with reference to Io. From all we have seen of our poet's repetition technique from *The Persians* onward, and particularly from the analogies in the *Oresteia,* it seems fair to conclude that Aeschylus did not incorporate these phrases in *Prometheus Bound* merely haphazardly, but that he designed them as pointers to an ultimate deliverance from sorrow in the *Prometheia* as a whole—certainly, as even the text of the extant play seems to prove, to the deliverances of the divine Prometheus and the human Io, very probably (as at the end of the *Oresteia*) the deliverance of all the parties to this conflict that, as the end of the extant play shows, is threatening the unity of the cosmos.

Not much more evidence about the outcome of the *Prometheia* can be obtained from *Prometheus Bound.* Henceforth we depend only on fragments: the quite numerous ancient quotations from *Prometheus Unbound,* which was evidently the immediate sequel to the *Bound,* and the pitifully few that survive from *Prometheus Pyrphoros* ("Fire-Carrier"), which many students conjecture to have been the third tragedy of a trilogy by Aeschylus on the Prometheus theme. If there ever was a satyr-play to conclude the group, no information at all has survived about it. What evidence the fragments can offer, however, is worth surveying briefly (the major verbatim fragments are given in S 104–14 and 118; translations of all the significant ones, with comment, may be found in the appendix to the Scully-Herington translation of *Prometheus Bound*, mentioned in the Epilogue).

Fantastic shapes loom out of the fragments of the *Unbound*. The opening of this play revealed Prometheus, now restored to the light and savaged by the eagle as Hermes had threatened. To him entered a chorus of Titans, no less; evidently by now this older generation of heavenly rulers had been released from the pit of Tartarus into which Zeus had cast them after their defeat (*Prometheus Bound* 219–21), and that release in itself may be interpreted as a sign that a different aspect of Zeus was emerging into view even as the *Unbound* opened. Then the evidence allows us a momentary glimpse only of a character who, so far as I know, was never again to tread the stage until the time of Wagner—namely, Earth. On the other hand, many quotations from a scene or scenes in which Io's descendant Herakles appeared survive. Like Io, Herakles was in the midst of a long and fearsome journey across the world, imposed on him by Hera's jealousy (he had been born of another of Zeus's passions for a mortal woman, Alcmene), and, again like Io, he received from Prometheus a prophecy about his future wanderings. His journey, too, it appeared from the prophecy, was destined to end gloriously, for he would reach the magical garden of the Maidens of the West, the Hesperides, where grew the tree with fruits of gold; at the last, according to all versions of his legend, he would join the Olympians as a god. Herakles in the *Prometheia*, then, like Prometheus and Io—and like Orestes in the *Oresteia*—was seen painfully following a path that led from present torment to ultimate peace and fulfillment. One may well think back, at this point, to the intuition expressed by the old men of *Agamemnon*'s chorus in the Zeus Hymn (above, pp. 121–22):

> And do the Spirits who sit at the august helm
> Through violence show their kindness?

Perhaps one may even think forward to a similar intuition into life's workings, arising though it does from an utterly different milieu: *dia pathēmatōn teleiōsai*, "to make perfect through sufferings" (*Epistle to the Hebrews* 2 : 10).

The fragments allow us to learn of only two further events that were either enacted or reported in the *Unbound*, but both seem of great importance to our understanding of the drift of the *Bound* and of the entire *Prometheia*. At some point before Herakles left to pursue his long westward journey, he shot Prometheus' tormentor, the eagle sent from Zeus (S 113). After that—how long after, we do not know—Zeus was reconciled with Prometheus, and released him. That is a certain inference from a passage in one of the most learned of ancient Greek writers, Athenaeus (M 334; S 128, footnote). Athenaeus tells us nothing of the plot mechanics through which the reconciliation was achieved, but he does mention that according to Aeschylus in *Prometheus Unbound* the human custom of wearing garlands (as the Greeks universally did at parties and festivals) was instituted "in honor of Prometheus . . . as a recompense for his chains." That information seems very significant in the light of all we have so far learned about Aeschylus' patterned imagery. The technique apparently used in the *Unbound* in order to culminate (visually?) the ultimate turning of Prometheus and Zeus toward each other may recall, for instance, the technique applied to show the ultimate turning of the Furies and the Olympians toward each other in *The Eumenides*. There the black costumes that throughout had symbolized the inexorable hostility of the dark powers toward the light were replaced by crimson, in token of great joy for all the people of Athens. In the Prometheus plays, it seems, the adamantine chains that had so long symbolized the inexorable "tyranny of Zeus" (*Bound* 10, 357) over the benefactor of humanity were replaced by chains of leaves or flowers, to be worn ever after by mortals at their revels.

That wonderfully joyous event marks the furthest point in the progress of the *Prometheia* that we are able to see now. The fragments of what may have been its final play, *Prometheus Pyrphoros*, reveal only that its action was set at some time later than the unbinding of Prometheus. Its title of "Fire-Carrier" might provoke our imaginations, perhaps, into a vision of a second bringing of fire, and all that fire means for the progress of civilization, to a rejoicing humanity, this time by the will of Zeus. But who can know what the imagination of Aeschylus might or might not have envisioned? On the evidence that we actually have, the *Prometheia* must remain, for us, the mere ruin of a masterpiece: perhaps Aeschylus' last, certainly his most spectacular masterpiece in that art developed during his latest years, which is neither quite tragedy nor quite comedy by any later definitions, but rather a drama of monstrous symbols, enacting both the crisis and the hopes of an Athens in abrupt transformation.

Yet history, too, has her paradoxes, and those no less breathtaking than the paradoxes of Aeschylean drama. The *Prometheia*'s one surviving complete play, through the very accident of mutilation, has probably exerted more influence on the subsequent course of Western ideas than it would ever have done had it been preserved in its original context. *Prometheus Bound* in isolation was practically certain to be read by postclassical generations, and in fact was read, as a signal for rebellion: rebellion of the intellectual and the technologist, on behalf of suffering humanity, against the relentless despotism of king or God. To the Byzantine scribes, that idea was simply unthinkable treason and blasphemy (some of them have left little poems in their manuscripts of *Prometheus Bound* expressing their outrage against both Prometheus and the poet who created him), and to many subsequent Christian editors it was a cause for scandal, or at least suspicion. Only in the Romantic period could the apparent message of the play be welcomed. In its depths poets and philosophers alike now read atheism and revolution, the liberation of the toiling masses from the tyranny of God and of the royal courts of Europe—ideas (so it appeared) conceived millennia before their time by one of the most revered of the classical poets, and proclaimed with the authority of genius. Even to this day it is hard for any student of *Prometheus Bound* to free himself altogether from the memory of Shelley's *Prometheus Unbound* (which culminates in a kind of cosmic Soviet) or of the teachings of Marxism (thanks to which, as much as to any other cause, our play may be read in postrevolutionary Russian and Chinese translations). Many other thinkers have created, and will surely create in future, their own sequels to *Prometheus Bound*, not only in books but also in society at large. All that is as it should be. Yet the hints contained within the play itself, and the evidence of the fragmentary plays of its group, seem to prove that in fact the *Prometheia* as it originally stood complete can have urged neither atheism nor revolution. Arising, like the *Oresteia*, out of the desperate political and intellectual dilemma of Aeschylus' city, it seems, again like the *Oresteia*, to have favored no extremes, but to have urged the redirection of all energies, male and female, innovative and conservative, intellectual and practical, from destructive mutual conflict toward a creative harmony.

In the *Prometheia* our poet seems directly to have faced

the impact of the new philosophy, science, and technology on the age-old archaic way of life, with all that it was to mean for high-classical Greek civilization—and for us too, of whom the poet Alberto de Lacerda has said:

Filhos cegos dos gregos,
a noite de seu Dia é que nos vê.

Blind children of the Greeks,
It is the night of their Day that looks at us.

Yet even at this late moment in his career Aeschylus did not desert the language of the myths, nor forget what the later Greeks, and we, were to forget for so long: that archaic sense of unity, of the coherence between the elements, the gods, the landscape, and humanity. On the contrary, in the *Prometheia* all those powers that together make up your universe and mine appeared from the beginning on the stage, manifested and interacting in ways only to be paralleled in the climaxes of his other dramas. In this majestic masque, set on a lonely peak high above the sea at the far end of the world, we have watched Ocean, Earth, the nymphs of the waters, Hephaistos, Hermes, Power, Violence, Io, and Herakles all pass to and fro before our eyes. Aeschylus presented those forces equally vividly in the verbal poetry also, in the Chorus' song at lines 397–435, in the tempestuous finale, and perhaps most wonderfully in Prometheus' opening words at the moment when he has been left in his chains, utterly alone (lines 88–92):

Splendor of the deep Sky, and winging Winds,
And springing Rivers, and unnumbered smiles
Of Ocean's waves, and Earth, mother of all;
You too I invoke, all-seeing orb of Sun:
See what a God can suffer from the Gods!

BIBLIOGRAPHICAL
EPILOGUE

A<small>NYONE WHO STUDIES AESCHYLUS AT THIS LATE TIME OWES HIS</small>
first thanks to many generations of earlier students, ranging
from Euripides and Aristophanes in the fifth century B.C.,
through the scholars of the Alexandrian Library and the Byzantine scribes and commentators, to the scholars of many nations who have continued the work of emending and
illuminating the texts from the High Renaissance to the present day. I wish to acknowledge that general obligation here
because a survey of Aeschylean drama that is to be of man-
ageable length can neither include their names nor—and this
is perhaps even more regrettable—discuss and weigh their
opinions and the reasons they have advanced to justify them.
Even the textual foundation of our plays is unusually precar-
ious; add to that the uniqueness, the almost boundless orig-
inality, of Aeschylean song, and it should surprise no one that
scarcely a phrase has escaped learned debate in the course of
the centuries, or that the interpretation and even the authenticity of entire dramas have evoked near-mortal controversy.
I have familiarized myself with as much as I can of this long
literary and philological dialogue, and have tried to test its
results, over many years, against the original plays in their
original language, delivering speech and song aloud and plot-
ting movements on a model of the Theater of Dionysus. From
the scholars and the texts together I have built up the picture
of Aeschylean drama that is presented in this book. If I was

to do justice to the inmost nature of the plays (as I, at least, had come to conceive it), it seemed necessary above all to remove them utterly from the study and the library and to view them as live performances in rhythmic sound and movement, enacted at the heart of one of the livest audiences in history at an epoch almost unparalleled to this day in the speed and gravity of the changes that it witnessed. Thus, given the scale and aims of the volumes planned for the Hermes series, there was no room left for detailed justification of the conclusions here adopted. I hope, however, that none of them has been reached without due consideration of divergent scholarly views.

I have at least tried to keep the reader informed of the evidence in the Aeschylean texts on which any given statement depends. Line references to the extant plays follow the numeration of the most recent critical edition, *Aeschyli Septem Quae Supersunt Tragoediae*, by Denys Page (Oxford, 1972). The same numeration, with occasional minor variations, is indicated by all the translators of Aeschylus who will here be mentioned. The reader who knows no Greek, or only a little, and wishes to come as close as possible to the literal meaning of Aeschylus, will do best to consult the edition by Herbert Weir Smyth, *Aeschylus*, 2 vols. (Cambridge, Mass., and London: Loeb Classical Library, 1922 and 1926). (It has often been reprinted since; the reprints of volume 2 from 1957 onward include an appendix, edited by Hugh Lloyd-Jones, which contains the major papyrus fragments of Aeschylus that came to light later than Smyth's original publication of his work.) This offers a faithful prose translation, with facing Greek text.

Translations into English verse, of which there have been very many since the latter half of the eighteenth century, are inevitably less literal and more subjectively colored than Smyth's; the best of them, however, perform the irreplaceable function of reminding us constantly that Aeschylus' work is not just drama but poetic drama. A verse translation of the *Oresteia* that is remarkable at once for its sensitivity and its close approach to literalness is Richmond Lattimore's, *Aeschylus I: Oresteia* (Chicago, *Complete Greek Tragedies*, 1959); somewhat freer, but perhaps conveying something more of the original's spiritedness, is Robert Fagles's *Aeschylus: The Oresteia* in the *Penguin Classics* series (1977). (This edition also offers much aid to the reader in the form of a long introduction, bibliography, notes, and glossary.)

The four extant plays that do not form part of the *Oresteia* have all been translated fairly recently by a group of American poets and scholars in collaboration, with introductions, notes, and glossaries, as part of *The Greek Tragedy in New Translations* series (London and New York): *The Seven Against Thebes* by Anthony Hecht and Helen H. Bacon (1973); *The Suppliants* by Janet Lembke (1975); *Prometheus Bound* by James Scully and John Herington (1975); *The Persians* by Janet Lembke and John Herington (1982). The fragments of Aeschylus's lost plays have never been translated in their entirety, although volume 2 of Smyth's edition, with Lloyd-Jones's appendix, gives translations of almost all the verbatim fragments that are one line or more in length. Where possible, I have referred to this collection, using the letter "S" followed by Smyth's fragment number. For the other ancient information relating to the lost plays, such as fragments less than a line long, and allusions or descriptions that do not cite Aeschylus verbatim, I have referred to the virtually complete collection (in the original languages) by Hans Joachim Mette, *Die Fragmente der Tragödien des Aischylos* (Berlin, 1959), using the letter "M" with Mette's fragment number.

The work by Antonin Artaud referred to in chapter 1 and elsewhere was published in Paris (1938) under the title *Le*

Théâtre et son double; my quotations are taken from the English translation by Mary Caroline Richards, *The Theater and Its Double* (New York, 1958). The couplet by Alberto de Lacerda, quoted near the end of my final chapter, will be found in *77 Poems, Translated by Alberto de Lacerda and Arthur Waley* (London, 1955), pp. 50–51. The reader who wishes to inquire further into the present state of scholarly opinion on Aeschylus' works, and into their historical and artistic background, may be referred in the first instance to the following books; all contain references to many other modern studies on their various topics.

Oliver Taplin's *The Stagecraft of Aeschylus* (Oxford, 1977) treats in detail not only this important aspect of our poet's art but also many questions of text and interpretation. *The Art of Aeschylus,* by Thomas G. Rosenmeyer (Berkeley and Los Angeles, 1982), offers a comprehensive survey of its subject; I would particularly recommend its bibliographies on each individual play (pp. 381–84) to anyone who may wish to follow up certain major questions which are rightly the subject of serious debate among students of Aeschylus, but which have of necessity been dealt with summarily in the present book. The most notable of them concern: the text, staging, and general interpretation of the Shield Scene in *The Seven Against Thebes* and the authenticity of the finale (lines 1005–78) of the same play; the assignment of speaking and singing roles, and the stage situation generally, in *The Suppliants* 825–902; and the authenticity of *Prometheus Bound.* This last problem has been discussed with particular heat during recent years. All informed parties to the debate agree that the play shows certain stylistic and metrical features that are not paralleled in the other surviving plays of Aeschylus, but opinion is divided as to whether these should be taken as sufficient proof of spuriousness or as yet another manifestion of our poet's spectacular versatility. That question cannot be said to have been settled, and indeed some may think it insoluble: by what scientific method can one define the stylistic or metrical capacity of a poet of this stature? On the other hand, it may have appeared from the present book that the major themes of *Prometheus Bound*, and the treatment of those themes, are entirely consistent with the themes and treatments observable elsewhere in the later group of Aeschylus' plays. On such evidence as we have, it has seemed reasonable to me to accept the ancient attribution of *Prometheus Bound* to our poet—an attribution which in fact was never questioned by anybody until about a century ago.

For a short but authoritative account of what is now known about the physical aspect of the Athenian theater, one may consult Erika Simon's *The Ancient Theater* (London and New York, 1982). J. J. Pollitt, in *Art and Experience in Classical Greece* (Cambridge, 1972), especially in the second chapter, excellently characterizes the momentous revolution that was taking place in the visual arts during the later decades of Aeschylus' life. Finally, the political history of Athens from the regime of Pisistratus to the establishment of the Periclean democracy is traced in book III and book IV, chapter 1 of N. G. L. Hammond's *A History of Greece to 322 B.C.*, 2d ed. (Oxford, 1967).

TABLE OF DATES

The titles of the extant plays of Aeschylus are here printed in capital letters.

Dates B.C.

ca. 534 Contests in *tragoidia* established at the Great Dionysia Festival in Athens.

ca. 525 Birth of Aeschylus.

510 Expulsion of the Pisistratid tyrants from Athens.

ca. 507 Institution of the Cleisthenic democracy.

ca. 498 Aeschylus first competes in the tragic contests.

490 The first Persian expedition sent to Greece, against Eretria and Athens; its defeat by the Athenians at Marathon.

Aeschylus fights in the battle of Marathon.

484 Aeschylus wins his first victory in the tragic contests.

480–479 The Persian invasion of Greece, led by King Xerxes: battles of Thermopylae and Salamis (480); battle of Plataea (479).

Aeschylus is present at the battle of Salamis.

472 Aeschylus wins first prize with his tetralogy, *Phineus, PERSIANS, Glaukos of Potniai,* and the satyr-play *Prometheus Pyrkaeus.*

At some period between this production and 468, he visits Sicily.

468 Sophocles first competes in the tragic contests, and defeats Aeschylus.

467 Aeschylus wins first prize with his tetralogy, *Laius, Oedipus, SEVEN AGAINST THEBES,* and the satyr-play *Sphinx.*

ca. 463–458 Pericles' rise to power in Athens; reform of the Areo-
            pagus, alliance with Argos, and establishment of the
            Periclean democracy.

   463(?) Aeschylus wins first prize with his tetralogy, *SUP-
          PLIANTS, Aigyptioi, Danaides,* and the satyr-play *Amy-
          mone.* (The date 463 is probable but not certain; at any
          rate, the production must have occurred in one of the
          years 466–459).

      458 Aeschylus wins first prize with his tetralogy, *AGA-
          MEMNON, LIBATION-BEARERS, EUMENIDES,* and
          the satyr-play *Proteus* (the group as a whole was later
          known as the *Oresteia*). Not long afterward he leaves
          Athens for Sicily.

Not externally dated, but probably, on stylistic grounds, to be dated
            very late in Aeschylus' life are his tragedies *PROME-
            THEUS BOUND, Prometheus Unbound,* and perhaps
            Prometheus Pyrphoros (modern students often refer to
            the group collectively as the *Prometheia,* although this
            title has no ancient authority).

    456/5 Death of Aeschylus at Gela in Sicily.

      455 Euripides first competes in the tragic contests.

INDEX

Absurd, Theater of the, 13
Achilles, 55–56, 157–58, 169
Aegisthus, 112–14 passim, 119, 120, 129–32 passim
Aeschylus: birth of, 15, 17; first production of, 16, 17; legend of his poetic inspiration by Dionysus, 17–18; at Marathon, 22, 30; death of, 25, 30, 31; later career of, 27–31
Agamemnon: in *Agamemnon*, 112–13, 115, 119, 124; in the *Iliad*, 157–58
Agamemnon, 45, 111–24, 125, 131–33 passim, 166, 168, 172, 174; first production of, 29–30; Tapestry Scene in, 39–40, 119–20, 155; verbal poetry of, 114–16; prologue in, 116–18, 129, 156; moral confusion in, 111, 119, 120–21; "Hymn to Zeus" in, 120–23
Aigyptioi, 101, 104
Aitnaiai, 28, 50–51
Ajax, 56–57
Amphiaraus, 87, 88
Amymōnē, 103; male and female in, 103, 104
Anaxagoras, 25–27, 149
Antigone (Sophocles), 84
Aphrodite: her speech in the *Danaides*, 102, 103, 124, 153
Apollo, 89, 91–92, 93, 128, 137, 139, 140, 142, 147, 150, 151; sanctuary of, at Delphi, 6, 79, 139; as son of Zeus, 6, 135; on human conception, 26–27, 147–48; warning of, to Laius, 79; command of, to Orestes,

125–26, 132; on Athena's conception, 135–36, 148
Areopagus, 24, 137, 146, 148–50 passim
Argus, 96, 97
Aristophanes, 41, 54–55
Aristotle, 20, 32, 41, 149
Artaud, Antonin, 13–14, 50, 138–39
Atē, 74–75
Athena, 142–45 passim, 148, 150; sanctuary of, 6, 18, 142, 145; as daughter of Zeus, 6; attributes of, 143, 145; speeches of, in *The Eumenides*, 149, 152, 153–55
Athenaeus, 35, 174
Athens: transition in, 15–27, 31, 110, 111, 136–37, 142, 147, 163; Periclean reforms in, 24–26, 63, 146, 148–49; in *The Eumenides*, 143–46, 148–49, 151
Atreus, 113, 114
Auditorium, 33, 34
Aulos, 35

Bacchae, The (Euripides), 84
Belus, 96, 97

Calchas, 121
Capaneus, 85
Cassandra, 112, 113, 120, 151
Cilissa, 129–30
Choreography (of Aeschylus), 54–55
Chorus, 35, 37, 41, 98–99
Cleisthenes, 20, 24
Clytaemnestra, in *Agamemnon*, 112–13, 115, 118–20, 123–24; as repre-